D0423042

BOOM

BOOM

Marketing to the Ultimate Power Consumer—the Baby Boomer Woman

Mary Brown and Carol Orsborn, Ph.D.

Foreword by Paco Underhill

AMACOM

AMERICAN MANAGEMENT ASSOCIATION

New York · Atlanta · Brussels · Chicago · Mexico City
San Francisco · Shanghai · Tokyo · Toronto · Washington, D.C.

Special discounts on bulk quantities of AMACOM books are available to corporations, professional associations, and other organizations. For details, contact Special Sales Department, AMACOM, a division of American Management Association, 1601 Broadway, New York, NY 10019.
Tel.: 212-903-8316. Fax: 212-903-8083.
Web Site: www.amacombooks.org

This publication is designed to provide accurate and authoritative information in regard to the subject matter covered. It is sold with the understanding that the publisher is not engaged in rendering legal, accounting, or other professional service. If legal advice or other expert assistance is required, the services of a competent professional person should be sought.

Library of Congress Cataloging-in-Publication Data

Brown, Mary
Boom : marketing to the ultimate power consumer—the baby boomer woman / Mary Brown and Carol Orsborn ; foreword by Paco Underhill.
p. cm.
Includes bibliographical references and index.
ISBN-10: 0-8144-7390-3
ISBN-13: 978-0-8144-7390-0
1. Women consumers. 2. Consumer behavior. 3. Marketing. 4. Baby boom generation. I. Orsborn, Carol. II. Title.
HC79.C6B76 2006
658.8'34082—dc22

2006010294

© 2006 Mary Brown and Carol Orsborn.
All rights reserved.
Printed in the United States of America.

This publication may not be reproduced, stored in a retrieval system, or transmitted in whole or in part, in any form or by any means, electronic, mechanical, photocopying, recording, or otherwise, without the prior written permission of AMACOM, a division of American Management Association, 1601 Broadway, New York, NY 10019.

Printing number

10 9 8 7 6 5 4 3

To all those who view marketing to the Baby Boomer woman not simply as an initiative, but rather as an intrinsic part of doing business.

CONTENTS

CONTENTS

FOREWORD

The executive is on a lunchtime mission: to pick out the perfect $60,000 diamond ring from De Beers on Fifth Avenue. The search is on for the size, shape, and quality that says "You deserve the very best."

And so it is that *she* finds and purchases the perfect ring for *herself,* places it on her own right hand, and reminds marketers in a broad range of industries that when it comes to the women of the Baby Boomer generation, we're on revolutionary ground.

For many years, marketers have been largely missing the boat when it comes to Baby Boomer women. The time is ripe for a book that takes marketing to this segment of the population seriously. This book's challenge to the marketing community is to wake up and rethink just who it is that has control over the economic purse strings.

This challenge should come as no surprise. Women 40+ are

accustomed to defying marketer's expectations. Not only have the women of the Baby Boomer generation established themselves as the primary purchasing agents for their families but, as the vignette above illustrates, these women are the first generation who have been given permission to spend money on themselves. In the historical model, the man spent his money and the women spent the family's money. In 2006, Boomer women not only have their own money—they have a lot of money.

Marketers can succeed with Baby Boomer women by embracing their uniqueness and following their dollars to where they are most likely to be spent. The best way to get at this is by observing her life stage needs. The woman purchasing the ring is likely to be a woman at the younger end of the Baby Boomer demographic, one of the first generation of women who have had permission to not go the traditional route of marrying and having children.

At the same time, for the leading edge of the demographic—women in their 50s and up—experience and matters of the spirit become more important than material items. After their children have left the nest, for example, many Baby Boomers are attracted to downsizing. They divest their homes and move to urban areas where they can walk to shopping and cultural activities. When they shop, they already have the basics covered. Now, these Boomer women are more likely to spend their money on things that will enhance or add value—or that help them to simplify their lives.

As women of this generation become less concerned about having "things," they become more focused on health and comfort. No longer victims of fashion, they have become used to being, and are self-confident in, who they are. You see this captured in the "real curves" movement, with some manufacturers and retailers waking up to the fact that there are more women who are size 12 than 2. Recently, we were invited to observe how older women shop differently for lingerie than do women in their 20s or 30s. Young women tend to buy lingerie as a fashion statement. Older women buy it as a staple. They are looking for comfort and support.

Housing provides another opportunity to cater to her changing needs. Builders in both urban and suburban environments, for example, should be aware of the fact that the largest and fastest-growing market for housing is nontraditional groupings of individuals, including aging women living communally as housemates. In an era where houses are universally designed around the single master bedroom, the savvy builder will construct houses with multiple master bedrooms.

And then there are shoes. Shopping for shoes hasn't drastically changed in fifty years. The woman looks at the shoes. The salesperson retrieves her selection from the back to present to her. In this sales transaction, getting the customer seated is key. And here is where, for women 50+, the system breaks down. In many cases, the chairs are too low. What 50-year-old customer wants to squat to try on shoes? Give her a comfortable seat, and she'll buy the shoes.

Whether it's housing, shoes, or diamond rings, make it clear to her that she belongs in your store, housing development, or office. Then follow the money.

Carol and Mary have a good story to tell—just read on.

—Paco Underhill

Paco Underhill is the founder of Envirosell (www.envirosell.com), a New York-based research and consulting firm with offices around the world. Underhill has spent more than twenty-five years conducting research on the different aspects of shopping behavior, earning his status as a leading expert and pioneer in the field. Underhill is a regular contributor to NPR and BBC Radio. His columns and editorials have appeared in the *New York Times*, the *Wall Street Journal*, and the *Christian Science Monitor*. His first book, *Why We Buy: The Science of Shopping* has been published in thirty languages. His second book, entitled *Call of the Mall: The Geography of Shopping*, was released in February 2004 by Simon & Schuster.

AUTHORS' NOTE

Contributing authors have provided case histories and commentary based on their personal and professional experience. Within their submissions, we have relied upon them in regard to accuracy of facts. When requested, we have honored their desire to safeguard proprietary information by fictionalizing certain details. Their opinions are their own and do not necessarily reflect the opinions of Mary Brown, Carol Orsborn, or Imago Creative. Some of the material in this book has appeared previously in *Femail Focus*, the Imago Creative e-newsletter, and on Imago Creative's website www.ImagoCreative.com.

Some of the authors' research material has been derived from *The Silver Pearl: Our Generation's Journey to Wisdom* (Ampersand Press, 2005) by Drs. Carol Orsborn and Jimmy Laura Smull, and from *The Wisdom Years: Women of the Baby Boomer Generation and Their Search for Meaning* by Drs. Carol Orsborn and Jimmy Laura Smull, presented at the fall colloquium for UCLA's Center for the Study of Religion, October 5, 2005, Los Angeles, California.

ACKNOWLEDGMENTS

With gratitude to our editor, Ellen Kadin, a kindred spirit who supported us every step through this project and who made sure we got in some good laughs, as well. Also, thank you to our masterful team at AMACOM: Rosemary Carlough, Jenny Wesselmann, Andy Ambraziejus, Lydia Lewis, Kama Timbrell, Therese Mausser, Penny Anna Makras, Erin Snyder, Mike Sivilli, Niels Buessem, Cathleen Ouderkirk, and Erica Buneo.

A special thank you to our contributing authors and especially to Paco Underhill for writing our foreword. You are men and women of vision, who are exercising a rare and valuable superpower: making the invisible visible.

Last but not least, our deep appreciation to the staff at Imago Creative, who rose to every occasion with style and grace. Special thanks to the in-house editorial staff—Alisa Conroy, Bill Morton, Alison Carrier, Hugh Brantner, and Laura Hnatow—who helped shepherd the best marketing minds in the country into our book.

Mary Brown:

Thanks to my husband, Hugh, and beautiful daughter, Olivia, whose support and love give me courage and light every day; to my vibrant mother, Molly Brown, who raised four talented, willful Baby Boomer daughters; and with respect and gratitude, to my coauthor, mentor, and wise woman, Carol Orsborn.

Carol Orsborn:

Thanks to the women in the Orsborn/Smull research study, and most of all, to Dr. Jimmy Laura Smull, who demonstrates beyond doubt that when it comes to becoming wise, time can be our greatest ally. Thanks also to my family: soul mate, Dan; first son, Grant; and first daughter, Jody; and to our growing network of significant others. And finally, a special thank you to my coauthor and Madam President, Mary Brown. You have the kind of courage and vision that it takes to change the world.

INTRODUCTION

She's the Emerging Power Consumer

We listened intently as the marketing research director of the major cruise line described his demographic focus to us for the coming year. "We recognized that 80 percent of the time, it's the woman who is making the major travel decisions for the family. As a result, we've decided to target women age 40 and under."

"Targeting women is a smart move," we said. "Women are going to control two-thirds of the consumer wealth in the United States over the coming decade. But is there any particular reason why you are targeting the age segment of the population that will see a 0 percent increase over the next few years while during the same period of time, the number of people age 45 to 64 will grow 30 percent?"[1]

The room suddenly grew quiet. After a brief pause, he shrugged his shoulders and smiled, "Perhaps we should revisit this."

Many marketers have come a long way since the days of automatically targeting the "demographic of choice," historically considered to be males between ages 18 to 34. Since the turn of this century, an increasing number of industries—and an even larger number of advertising, public relations, and marketing professionals—have come to recognize that there are demographic goldmines embedded in broad segments of the population just waiting to be tapped.

In our increasingly demanding marketplaces, many view appealing to previously under-represented segments of the population as critical to gaining the edge over less enterprising competitors. Marketing groups with specialized knowledge of the Hispanic, African-American, youth, or women segments, to name a few, have been rapidly springing up to meet the demands of the sophisticated marketer seeking expertise on issues of gender, age, ethnicity, and even religion. And like the research director of the cruise company, competitive marketers are more willing than ever to admit that in doing so, they often find themselves on largely unexplored terrain. For nearly everybody in the marketing field, this is an era of intense excitement, fueled as much by the adrenaline of trial and error as by the promise of the rewards. Many of those whose companies are willing to test the waters are already proving to be big winners. Others are going back to the drawing boards, learning from their mistakes.

A Prize Worth the Risk

The prize has to be worth the risk, and in the case of Baby Boomer women, the numbers promise that it is. Baby Boomers make up, at approximately 78 million, the largest generational demographic in history—and the majority of Baby Boomers today are women, a proportion that will increase substantially over the coming decades. Beyond their sheer numbers, Boomer households spend more every year on consumer goods and services than their younger cohorts. Additionally, with more established careers than younger generations, Boomer women are at the peak of their earning potential, with many planning to work well into their 60s, 70s, and beyond. Not only will they continue to earn income, but within the next decade, many Boomer women will be managing inheritance windfalls from their parents and husbands.

Happily, the cruise company hired us to consult with them on how to market successfully to women of the Baby Boomer generation. Just as importantly, out of this and many other encounters, we recognized the need for a practical, myth-busting book on the subject for marketers in a broad spectrum of industries. As we began sharing our vision, we also recognized the pent-up demand for a forum for those amongst us who are pioneering this new terrain, learning as we go. The result is the book you hold in your hands.

From the beginning, we felt it was important to give voice not just to our own insights and expertise. This moment in marketing history is not about any one individual's pronouncements, no matter how wise and perceptive she or he may be. Rather, we recognize that we are poised on the verge of no less than a marketing revolution: the traditional wisdom about population segments worth targeting turned virtually on its head. Women 40+, heretofore largely invisible in marketing circles, are becoming increasingly recognized as the powerhouse consumer.

Insider's Intelligence

Even more compelling than the numbers is the intelligence on what has and hasn't worked for the cutting-edge companies who have hands-on experience with Boomer women consumers. As marketers, we have been privileged to have a front-row seat, witnessing triumphs and misses—and most importantly, hearing the stories of these demographic pioneers.

Over the years, Imago Creative has partnered with clients in a wide range of industries, from fashion and food, to furniture and finance. Seeing the need for an area expert, Founder and President Mary Brown evolved Imago into the only strategic marketing firm in the United States specializing exclusively in helping companies build brand relationships with women 40+. We are additionally immersed in this emerging market by having developed Imago Creative.com, and through our e-newsletter, "Femail Focus," a leading online clearinghouse for marketing intelligence about women 40+. Our database and archival research gives us access to the best-of-class marketing efforts from a broad range of industries, with statistical support to back them up.

In addition to giving voice to our smart and courageous gathering of marketing experts, we recognized the need for progressive proprietary research to fill in the missing pieces of intelligence. As a research associate with UCLA, senior level strategist, and a 25-year public relations veteran, Dr. Carol Orsborn comes to this book with a unique academic and psychosocial perspective on marketing to the Baby Boomer woman.

Visionary Marketers

Together, we began identifying individuals, companies, and industries both in and beyond our own client base who have launched, or are in the process of launching, marketing initiatives targeted to women of the Baby Boomer generation. The response to our invitation to join this book as a contributing author has been tremendous, reflecting peaking interest among marketers and the public in this promising and largely underserved demographic. Each of our contributing authors was asked to respond to their choice of any one or combination of the following three questions:

1. Do you see an economic market opportunity in the sizable female Baby Boomer demographic for your industry? Do you think the marketplace as a whole has fully tapped this demographic's potential?

2. Have you seen (or been involved with) a particular ad campaign and/or marketing effort that has effectively communicated with Baby Boomer women? What tools or approaches do you think are or would be effective?

3. If you are a member of this generation, what personal requests/hopes/advice do you have concerning how you would like to see this group addressed? What kind of positive impact could this have on you, the business community, the world?

Missionary Zeal

As you will soon be discovering in the following pages, their answers to these questions—and more—are illuminating, to say the least. There is, indeed, the sense of discovery as individual marketers working independently from one another have been brought together in the context of this book to help connect the dots. The intelligence and wisdom they provide is as generous as it is welcome, as the opening of this new marketing frontier takes on a nearly missionary zeal. "This is an exciting time to be a marketer," says Melissa McVicker, director of Intel's Global Communications Group. "Our industry is just now beginning to look at Baby Boomer women as the burgeoning market segment it is. Some of us are doing a better job figuring it out than others. But ultimately, what it is about, is enriching this previously underrepresented consumer's life through innovative technology." The same sentiment was echoed by contributing authors in fields ranging from travel, automotive and financial services to healthcare, food, and apparel.

Throughout the book, you will be hearing from market leaders from a broad range of industries, who share what they've learned about how to connect effectively with this new power consumer. Incorporating proprietary cutting-edge research, the book provides practical guidance and motivational tools for marketers who want to build powerful brand relationships with women of the Baby Boomer generation.

What You'll Learn

In the pages ahead, you will have access to all the intelligence you need to:

- Develop a roadmap to increase your market share of today's most lucrative consumer
- Minimize the risks and maximize the potential of marketing to this challenging but promising demographic
- Know what industry leaders (and in many cases, the competition) are thinking/doing about marketing to Baby Boomer women
- Put your hands on the statistics and power points in order to sell others in your company on putting resources against this up-and-coming market segment
- Make strategic decisions about the messages and communications channels you choose to use with her

Given the range and depth of voices, perspectives, and research represented in these pages, this book promises not only to sound the starting bell for this emerging consumer powerhouse, but to be a definitive guide on the subject, with advice provided by some of the smartest minds in the business today. So buckle your seatbelts. After all, *She's* in the driver's seat!

CHAPTER ONE

She's the Sweet Spot

The New Demographic of Choice

Imagine walking into your local newsstand and seeing the majority of magazines featuring women 40+ on the cover and in their ads. In a world of marketing and media that has spent decades courting the 18- to 34-year-old male consumer as the demographic of choice, this may strike you as a far-fetched notion. But the truth is that it is the woman 40+ who is increasingly establishing herself as the power consumer of today. She is already making the majority of household purchases, spending well over a trillion dollars a year on consumer goods and services.[1] And now, as both her numbers and dollars continue to dominate the consumer marketplace, she's poised to turn the marketing world upside down.

We're talking here, of course, about the women of the Baby Boomer generation: the largest and most economically, socially, and politically powerful generation in the United States, as well as in many of the industrialized countries around the globe. There were more than 40 million Baby Boomer women born in the United States alone, between the years of 1946 and 1964.[2]

Raised self-aware of her power and potential, the Baby Boomer woman is not one who accepts invisibility or marginalization as an option. This mindset isn't changing, even as she enters the unmapped territory of her middle age and, just over the horizon, old age. The days of women 40+ being ignored by marketers and the media are numbered. In fact, the groundswell of growing awareness promises to be not only a sociological revolution, but a marketing one, as well—one that is literally flipping the demographic desirability chart on its head. Many companies are being pleasantly surprised by the discovery that Baby Boomer women are proving to be an unexpected consumer gold mine that had previously been overlooked.

On Marketing to Technology Optimists

Rose Rodd,

Director of Corporate Marketing

PALM, INC.

By 2002 Palm had won the hearts and minds of many business professionals, the majority of whom were affluent, male, and familiar with computer technology. Palm's goal was now to expand our customer reach by broadening our target, attracting more mainstream consumers who were less "techie" and more price conscious. Based on our research, we determined that the demographic segment with the greatest *emo-*

tional need for our products had previously barely been considered for PDA (Personal Data Assistant) ownership: busy women trying to balance numerous aspects of their lives and often on a budget. If designed and marketed properly, this new product would help Palm stand for a whole new way of living rather than just another way of keeping track of phone numbers and schedules. The Palm Zire was created to offer these women what they truly desired: a simpler life.

Almost immediately, the Zire (followed over the next several years by Zire 21, Zire 31, and Zire 72) captivated the target audience. By 2005, Palm's female customer base was up four- to five-fold over the rate in 2002. And we learned that the heaviest users of the Zire handheld were somewhat older than we expected: 35 to 55 years of age. At the core of this demographic were the women of the Baby Boomer generation.

One of the keys to our success with this demographic was the decision to sell the "real-world benefits" of the Zire organizer, not sell the "technology." That made all the difference for women who understood what an improvement the Zire would be over sticky yellow note-laden Filofaxes. Pricing was a key element to the success of this product given that it had to cost the same as a paper organizer in order to be considered an alternative. At $99—a one-spouse decision in many households—this strategy allowed us to introduce women to the product and then help them graduate up the product line in the future to more sophisticated models.

In naming our product to appeal to women, we dropped the Palm tradition of using Roman numerals (Palm V, Palm VII, and so on), and gave our new product an actual name—Zire. In our focus groups, women particularly resonated with the name Zire, making such aspirational comments as "Zire sounds like something I would covet," "Everything I desire at my fingertips," or "It's sleek, simple, hip, fun."

We also chose a new smaller, rounded clear plastic packaging design versus the former cardboard rectangular box, knowing that our customer would find it important to see how stylish, simple, and small the product is. Retailers liked it, too, because Zire was designed to hang from a peg and be more of a "grab and go" product. It was also the first time our packaging portrayed a bold image of the target customer.

When it came to marketing Zire, another first: Palm created a specifically female-focused campaign. A woman was the hero and communicated the thousands of ways Palm could touch and improve her life. At the same time, the campaign celebrated the strong emotional attachment long-time customers and "evangelists" already had with the Palm brand. It featured examples of how she could be less stressed, more capable, and "together" with a Palm Zire in hand.

Other firsts in the computer technology subcategory included running ads in magazines like *Real Simple, Better Homes & Gardens*, and *People* instead of the old standards focused on business and technology. We used radio and newspaper publicity to drive consumers to in-store product demos. This direct, one-on-one interaction proved very successful with women in terms of breaking down barriers to entry, reversing misperceptions about complexity and driving sales of the Zire product among women.

We also changed our channel distribution strategy adding new retailers, such as Target in the United States and Gigante, a large grocery chain in Mexico—quite a change from our former computer-superstore approach. And we tried a pilot stint on QVC, a TV shopping network. Applying the insight we gained from consumer focus groups, we communicated with customers in their preferred retail environments, using words they used, and we reached them with emotional messages. Women could be more confident and competent keeping their busy lives running smoothly with our products. On QVC, women who phoned in their orders were heard explaining how *they* planned to use it, reinforcing that the purchase was in fact for them and not for a man in their life. The result: About 3,000 Zire handhelds were sold in minutes.

This highly-targeted approach has now been applied to our other product lines with the potential for broader appeal, such as the Treo smartphone. There is high awareness for Palm products with women of the Boomer generation because of their exposure to handheld devices in the workplace. And while PDAs originally were attractive mostly to men, our most capable products—including the Palm Treo family of smartphones—enjoy increasing popularity among women, especially of the Baby Boomer generation. This demographic, once ignored by the consumer electronics industry is now a targeted segment by leading companies, including Palm, who fondly refer to this group as "Technology Optimists."

Rose G. Rodd is the director of corporate marketing for Palm, Inc., a world leader in mobile-computing products. Rose is responsible for the company's advertising, branding, and product launch planning. For the last five years, Rose has deepened the company's understanding of its customers and integrated those insights into Palm products, packaging, and promotional materials. As a result, the company has attracted a larger population of female customers. Rose spends much of her time at Palm understanding and optimizing the customer experience, which is key to Palm's brand promise, its market leadership and the company's overall success. Rose holds an MBA from the University of Michigan and a BS degree in communications from Northwestern University.

But it isn't only in the United States that the population surge following World War II made demographic waves. Japan, for example, also experienced a significant increase in population during the same period of time. As a result, Japanese companies are beginning to acknowledge that they, too, can no longer afford to ignore this segment of the population.[3] In Europe, Baby Boomer women are on the radar screen in such countries as France, Great Britain, and Italy. Other parts of the world, such as Australia and Canada, also experienced a boom. In fact, exceeding U.S. proportions, an astonishing one out of every three Canadians living today are members of the Baby Boomer generation.[4]

On Marketing to Baby Boomer Women in Canada

Anne-Marie Caron,

Marketing Manager

LIZ CLAIBORNE CANADA, YZZA, AND SIGRID OLSEN CANADA

Female Boomers are the fastest-growing demographic group not just in the United States, but also across the border in Canada where their numbers are climbing by almost 30 percent annually, and will continue at that pace until 2011. The amount of money Canadian women between the ages of 40 and 55 have spent on apparel over the past few years has risen by about 15 percent annually. Yet, this demographic has remained very underserved in Canada's fashion industry.

Similarly to their U.S. counterparts, Canada's Boomer

women are multitaskers, extremely busy juggling work and family, and very budget conscious. They also struggle with issues of aging, but remain young in attitude and outlook. Also similarly to the United States, Canada's fashion industry has been more focused on the younger demographics. Where Canada's retail industry does differ is that we have far fewer specialty stores. Department stores are much more prevalent. As a result, the Boomer woman's shopping options have been very limited. Furthermore, in Canada, shopping online is a less accepted shopping channel for her than for her American counterpart.

We decided to come up with a concept that would offer her great fashions (designed for her Boomer attitude and body), an appealing environment, and excellent customer service—really send the message that we understand her needs. With this vision, and with the tremendous resources available through Liz Claiborne Canada Ltd., we launched a new retail concept: Yzza (pronounced *ease-ah*). The first four stores opened in 2005, with plans to open another sixty locations within five years.

The response has been excellent. Women love that they can find clothes for work, for play, and for weekends all in one place at a great value. All the collections are coordinated so that if she buys one item now, and another one in several months, they still work together. We hire managers and sales staff who have the maturity she can relate to. The stores are very warm and inviting, like a living room. There is a fireplace and sitting areas where she can relax and read books or magazines of interest to her. The entrance is designed as a vestibule, so when she enters the store it feels like a home. Her life is so hectic, we want her shopping experience to be a part of her day when she can relax and have fun.

We're already seeing evidence of a strong customer loyalty to Yzza. We foster this with a loyalty rewards program in which we give (among other things) a discount on her birthday. We've seen groups of women making this birthday discount a social event. A group of them will go to lunch together and then go shopping at Yzza so the birthday gal can use her discount. Shopping can't get much more fun than that!

Anne-Marie Caron joined Liz Claiborne Canada in 2004 as marketing manager of its Missy Brands, which includes Liz Claiborne Canada, Yzza, and Sigrid Olsen. Prior to this position, Anne-Marie taught Consumer Behavior and Marketing Strategy at the Collège Marie-Victorin, well known for its fashion merchandising program. Her extensive background also includes marketing positions at fashion retailers Reitmans Canada and Mexx Canada (now known as Liz Claiborne Canada, Inc.). She holds a degree in fashion merchandising from Collège LaSalle and a bachelor's degree in marketing from École des Hautes Études Commerciales de Montréal.

The Convergence of Two Major Trends

This Baby Boomer woman marketing juggernaut is situated squarely on the convergence of two major trends. One trend centers around the relatively recent awareness of the growing influence women hold over all facets of the consumer economy. The second equally important trend is the impact of the huge Boomer population that is moving into the midlife and beyond stage previously populated by the smaller and less vocal "Silent Generation," also known as the "Ikes" named after one of their major influencers, the Eisenhower presidency.

These two trends have been fueled by the pressure upon marketers to respond to the post-recession demands of an increasingly competitive and consumer-driven marketplace. Feeling the heat globally, companies in many industrialized countries have been driven to seek and develop new demographic bases for their products and services. For example, in the United States, the economic potential of Hispanic, African-American, Asian, youth, gay, and conservative Christian consumer segments has spawned cadres of marketing specialists. These expert insiders are immersed and conversant in cultures that have previously been outside the marketing mainstream. In addition, many advertising, public relations, and marketing firms, as well as corporate in-house marketing departments themselves, have added demographic subculture specialists to their team.

The earlier of the two trends that grabbed marketers' attention was the rise of the female consumer. A number of marketing-to-women initiatives have been launched since the turn of the century in a broad range of industries. As in the case of Palm, Inc., the marketing-to-women initiatives were often geared at an either slightly, or in many cases, dramatically younger age group than the Baby Boomer segment of the marketplace. In fact, many of these initiatives, if not targeting teenagers and women in their early twenties, were centering around "marketing-to-moms" of young children. A number of our contributing authors attribute this fascination with the younger age group as a reflection of the fact that in many companies, the marketers themselves are Gen X or younger. Their perception of the size and influence of the percentage of the female demographic dealing with changing diapers and serving up alphabet soup is skewed by their own experiences and interests. This bias is giving way, however, bowing under the sheer weight of the statistical evidence as to where the real economic clout lies: Baby Boomer women.

The Generational Angle

Approaching 2006, as the first group of Baby Boomers began turning 60, the second demographic trend—the generational angle—

also came seriously into play. A growing number of marketers, of all ages and in a broad range of industries, began figuring out that Baby Boomers are a large and highly lucrative segment of consumers. Consider that, at 78 million strong, Boomers are far greater in number than the 50 million Gen Xers or the 70 million Gen Yers[5] (see Figure 1-1). By 2010, the population of 45- to 64-year olds will have grown 30 percent, compared to the stagnant growth of 25- to 44-year olds.[6] And a majority of this growth will be Boomer women, as women tend to outlive men.

Even beyond the sheer size of this demographic, Boomer households spend an additional $10,000 more every year on consumer goods and services than their younger cohorts.[7] To put this into context, adults 50+ will spend 2.5 times as much as younger consumers on a per capita basis.[8] By 2010, adults 45 and older, the majority of whom are women, will be outspending younger adults by $1.6 to $2.6 trillion.[9]

These two trends, marketing to women and marketing to Baby

Figure 1-1. U.S. population by generation.

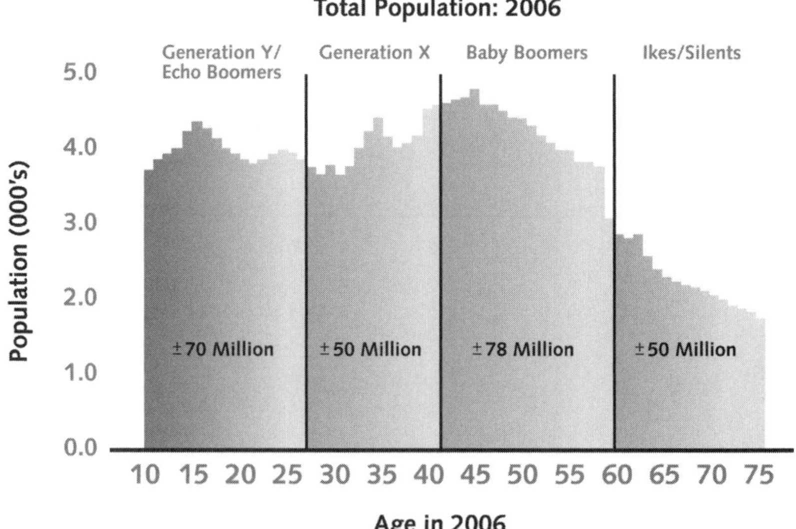

Figure 1-1 builds on a conceptual framework provided by the Mature Market Group, a division of J. Walter Thompson Worldwide, New York, 2004.

Boomers, have been independently gathering energy side-by-side, each cheered on by its own group of experts. But the realization is dawning among marketers in a broad range of industries that it's not really only women and not really only Baby Boomers that represent the biggest opportunity for the coming decade. Rather, it is where the two populations intersect that is the real "sweet spot": women of the Baby Boomer generation. The numbers and dollars are so impressive, in fact, that for many marketers this segment of the population is no longer perceived as a "niche"; rather, it has gone straight to the head of the demographic class.

Take a look at the following facts:

Seven Things You May Not Know About Boomer Women (But Should)

1. In the next decade, women will control two-thirds of the consumer wealth in the United States.[10] Boomer women make up the largest generational demographic of this purchasing powerhouse, currently influencing as much as 80 percent[11] of the $2.1 trillion Boomers spend on consumer goods and services.[12]

2. With more established careers than younger generations, many Boomer women are at the peak of their earning potential. What's more, eight out of ten Boomers say they don't plan to retire,[13] with an estimated 52 percent increase in the category of women 55+ projected for the work force by 2010.[14]

3. Not only will they continue to earn income, but within the next decade, many Boomer women will be managing inheritance windfalls from their parents and husbands. As the statistics reveal, they are likely to outlive their husbands on average of 6-9 years.[15]

4. Even in categories traditionally considered to be "male," it turns out that women are responsible for more than half the purchases.

They make 80 percent of home improvement decisions,[16] spend more than $55 billion annually on the $96 billion consumer electronics industry, account for 65 percent of all new automobiles sold every year, and purchase over 66 percent of computers.[17] Add on to all of this the fact that disposable incomes are highest for women age 45 to 54, and it becomes evident who is driving a majority of the numbers.[18]

5. In 2004, women age 35 to 54 represented the highest proportion of Web surfers, compared with male Boomers and all other demographics.[19] Direct catalog marketers calculate that 70 percent of all their online purchases are made by women, the majority of whom are in the Boomer demographic.[20]

6. Majority- and privately-owned women's firms number 6.7 million, and account for 30 percent of all small businesses in the country. This growth in firms is twice the rate of all U.S. companies.[21] Not only that, but 86 percent of female entrepreneurs say they use the same products and services at home as they do in their businesses.[22] This sub-segment skews heavily toward women age 35 to 54, with Baby Boomers making up 65 percent membership of one of the leading national women's business organizations.[23]

7. Do you think that these middle-aged women are set in their ways? Think again. According to the Center for Women's Business Research, almost seven in ten women over 35 years old (68 percent) say that the older they get, the more they enjoy trying new things.

In other words, Baby Boomer women are the greatest market opportunity today. There are quite simply more of them consuming more products and capable of flexing more combined social, economic, and political muscle than any other gender or age segment of the population. What's more, the Baby Boomer woman is continuing to both spend and work, and anticipates remaining a potent social and economic force well into her 70s and beyond. With state-of-the-art medical treatments, cosmetic advances, and healthier nutritional awareness, she looks and feels a good decade or more younger than her chronological age. Throwing off the old stereotypes of aging, this is a vital group of women who are simultaneously waking up to both the need and the potential to reinvent not only their own futures, but what it means to market a product or service to a woman over 40.

A Competitive Advantage

Investing in better understanding these women will provide companies with a competitive advantage in the marketplace of the future. And with Boomers turning 50 at the rate of one every seven to ten seconds, it's not a moment too soon. That's more than 12,000 each day and over 4 million a year spanning eighteen years.[24]

As marketers will tell you, it wouldn't matter how many women are in this demographic if the traditional marketing adages were true: that after 40, female consumers have already solidified their brand preferences. Jan DeLyser of the California Avocado Commission has had first-hand experience with this demographic, discovering that women of the Baby Boomer generation are not only open to new experiences, but are becoming increasingly "experimental" with age.

On Baby Boomer Women and Experimentation

Jan DeLyser,

Vice President of Marketing

CALIFORNIA AVOCADO COMMISSION

The Baby Boomer woman has been an important demographic for us for several decades, through numerous life stages. With the avocado market's expansion into new geographical areas, due in part to year-round product availability, the Baby Boomer woman is as important to us as ever, for a number of reasons. For example, through new market trials, we have learned that as a woman gets older, she becomes more willing to experiment with new foods, cuisines, and recipes. As a result, our target age for this new "experimental" consumer has been creeping up from 25 to 54, to a slightly older demographic, encompassing the Leading-Edge of Baby Boomers who are now turning 60. This is critical information, particularly when talking about introducing avocados to parts of the country, such as the Midwest, where consumers are less familiar with them.

There are aspects to avocados that are particularly appealing to Baby Boomer women. And there are challenges, as well. One challenge has to do with this generation's desire for immediate gratification. We have had to work with retailers to make sure that the avocado they sell to her is ready to eat today. Often, it's only as the Baby Boomer woman is driving home from work that she's thinking about what she will be fixing for dinner that night. She doesn't have the time to let the avocado ripen on her kitchen counter. More often than not, it will be an impulse buy and have to be ready to be consumed that evening.

Another challenge stems from the Baby Boomer woman's personal, as well as generational, nutritional history. When these women were younger, their attitudes about nutrition were largely formed by the anti-fat bias held in dietary circles. Avocado fat was lumped together with butter, cottonseed oil, and all the other fats, virtually without differentiation. Over time, nutritional advice concerning fats has become increasingly sophisticated. Interest in Mediterranean diets and olive oil has raised awareness that there are also other sources of beneficial mono-unsaturated fat, such as avocado oil, that can be part of a healthy diet.

To reposition avocados for the Baby Boomer woman who was raised on the negative fat message, we fuse the indulgence and nutritional messages to communicate to her that what she craves is okay to consume. Here's where positive associations come into play. We have worked hard to appeal to her on an emotional level, positioning the avocado as an acceptable indulgence for herself and her family. We invest in a strong outreach program to food writers, nutritionists, and online education resources, as the Baby Boomer woman pays attention to these credible, impartial sources. Expansion into new markets is succeeding as Boomer women respond to the notion that they can take care of themselves, eat something they want, and do it guilt-free.

Jan DeLyser has been with the California Avocado Commission since 1998 and manages the Commission's marketing functions including; consumer advertising, merchandising, public relations, nutrition, food service and the Internet. Her responsibilities include merchandising programs for the Chilean Avocado Import Association and management of all marketing functions for the Hass Avocado Board, a federal entity. Prior to joining the Commission, DeLyser spent twenty-two years in various facets of the produce industry, including trade publications, trade association management, marketing for an international agricultural company, and sales for a produce distributor. Jan was the recipient of the Fresh Produce and Floral Council's Southern California Produce Achievement Award in 2003.

She's Her Own Unique Demographic

If this convergence between women and Baby Boomers is so sweet, why have marketers been so slow to come to the table? The obvious first response to this question is that while the Baby Boomer woman bears many qualities and characteristics in common with both the female and the Baby Boomer demographic, it is the differences that make targeting her both rewarding—and challenging.

Throughout this book, our contributing authors pool their considerable brainpower to address how it is that as consumers, Baby Boomer women differ from Baby Boomer men, as well as how Baby Boomer women differ from women of other generations. Setting aside, for a moment, the fact that targeting women 40+ is such a new discipline, requiring at least a certain degree of both courage and vision on the part of the marketer, there are larger sociological forces at work. It is not accidental that males age 18 to 34 have held sway as the demographic de jour for as long as most of us can remember. But exactly where and how was it that women 40+ fell off the radar screen?

Surprisingly, one answer finds its roots in the years following World War II. You may recall from reading your history books that when the young men went off to war, women and older people were prevailed upon to play a vital role in keeping the country running. Rosie the Riveter rode to work every morning on a bus filled with women of all ages and men unable to serve in the military. Not only that, but they were competent to fill that role and happy to do so. These previously under-utilized populations aptly stepped into mainstream jobs traditionally held by younger men. This included physical jobs, such as working in the factories, as well as management and service industry positions. The country did just fine—and these hard-working civilians were applauded for their heroism on the home front, just as their young men were celebrated for the victory abroad.

Then the boys came home. Women and older workers (and older women, doubly so) were prevailed upon to patriotically step aside at war's end to make room for the returning soldiers. Those who failed to cooperate were labeled as cranky and eccentric. The "greatest generation" bought into this notion, viewing it as a given that young men be fully employed while women, the infirm, and the elderly graciously surrender their positions and retreat quietly to the margins.

The culturally-defined stereotypes of aging continued to be fed by a perfect storm of biology, politics, and economics. Living out the ramifications of what was to be a self-fulfilling prophecy, this was a generation where people were perceived as being old at 50. They looked old. They acted old. Mostly, the only individuals who even considered working past 65 were those who absolutely had to. The only future they faced was one in which a depressing decline was inevitable.

Busting the Stereotypes

The stereotypes persist.

And so it is that, when they were younger, the generation of Baby Boomers unwittingly bought into this notion of a depressing decline when they guiltlessly partook of a culture that equated youth with the capacity to make a contribution to society. And remember that old rock and roll battle cry teenage Boomers sang out so enthusiastically—not to trust anybody over 30? It is ironic that it was in large part the sheer size of this generation that established 18- to 34-year-olds as the marketer's dream during the decades following their coming of age in the late 1960s and beyond.

It is a further irony that as this generation outgrew its own adolescence, the focus on the teens and twenty-somethings they inspired, stayed put. By the time she was approaching menopause—and certainly thereafter—a woman was thought to have become an undesirable consumer for the vast majority of mainstream marketers. Not only did many companies believe that marketing to her would be a bother and a waste of time, but that by doing so, they would turn off the prized younger consumers, and men as well.

Baby Boomers, brainwashed by the marketing and advertising community's stereotypes of aging, fully expected to enter into this vast wasteland of old age, epitomized by the Beatle's famous ditty on turning 64. Now that the chronological date on their drivers' license says they've arrived, Baby Boomers are suddenly waking up to a starkly different reality. The depressing decline did not set in at 40 or 50, and with 60-year-olds like Tina Turner, Bob Dylan, Paul McCartney, and Mick Jagger jumping around on the world stage, the notion of "senior citizen" has already fallen somewhere on the spectrum between quaint and laughable. Clearly, this is not their parents' midlife and beyond.

Adult Development Models Playing Catch-Up

It wasn't only the Baby Boomers and marketers who have been caught by surprise by the notion of 40+ being a time of continued, or even renewed, vitality. Even in academic circles, the concept of ongoing psychosocial growth is challenging the older notions of adult development. Until recently, the period of midlife and beyond in a woman's life was considered to be, at most, a footnote to where the real action lies: in childhood, adolescence, and early adulthood.

The classical developmental theorists such as Jean Piaget fed this by arguing that one's full intellectual potential will have been basically determined by the time one reaches adolescence. Scholar Lawrence Kohlberg focused on the moral development in male children and adolescents, asserting that people reach their peak level at around the age of 16. In the view of these early life theorists, people at midlife and beyond are perceived as primarily passive recipients of their early childhood influences and predispositions—but after adolescence, at most harvesters and no longer creators of their destinies.

Developmental pioneer Erik Erikson was among the first to propose stretching the boundaries of theory to cover the entire lifespan of the individual. However, even Erikson's notion of eight life-stages casts the mature individual in a largely passive role. For Erikson, the fulfillment of one's potential culminates with stepping out of the way shortly after midlife to allow the next generation to come into its own. Ironically, as Erikson himself aged, he was quickly revising his stages as he went. In his last book, collaborating with wife Joan, he added a ninth stage to acknowledge that psychological and spiritual development could grow in strength and vitality throughout one's life.

In a follow-up book, *Wisdom and the Senses*, written when she was well into her 80s, Joan Erikson summarized their revolutionary late-in-life realization: "The whole earth, the planet, the cosmos, is in a state of constant change. We are all and with everything, involved in a process."

New Research Fills in the Gaps

Applying original research by Drs. Carol Orsborn and Jimmy Laura Smull to the subject,[25] our findings reflect Joan's personal experience, echoed by the majority of women in our study: namely, that personal growth and spiritual development are anticipated by many

Baby Boomers to have the potential of continuing all of their lives. The study begins to fill in the gaps of traditional adult development theory. Our findings point the way to an opportunity for marketers to tap into this surprisingly dynamic demographic throughout the course of their adult lives. In the words of one Boomer woman research participant: "In many ways, the best has been saved for last."

Far from buying into the belief that their power was destined to diminish as they aged, the majority of women in our study experienced themselves as gathering strength in regards to the issues, qualities, and characteristics that mattered most to them. While not denying that there are issues associated with aging, they are confident that they have the capacity to handle whatever it is that life brings their way. They are, after all, the generation that has approached every life stage and challenge on their path, not as barriers to reaching their goals, but as problems to be solved. This is the generation that rose up against the mythology that defined the perfect woman of the 1950s, and out of their convictions and enthusiasm, birthed the women's liberation movement. And that was only the beginning. As young adults, they took on a wide array of institutions, including politics and religion. Establishing their careers, they defied the experts by showing that it was possible, if challenging, to balance work and parenting, inventing their own version of having it all.

Now, they've turned their focus to tackling the issues that are arising for them at midlife and beyond. For instance, in the 1950s, they grew up in families in which their mothers were ashamed of "the change" and other physical challenges related to aging. The women of the Baby Boomer generation have transformed "hot flashes" into "power surges," using markers of aging as occasions for personal and communal empowerment. "Menopause the Musical®", a 90-minute celebration of aging, reports that over six million women have attended the show, motivated almost entirely by woman-to-woman word-of-mouth. (We will revisit this marketing phenomenon in greater depth in Chapter Six.)

Beyond Walls of Shame

To make a long story short, women are refusing to be ashamed of their ages and life changes. A seminal moment for this quiet revolution may actually have a specific time, date, and place: December 6, 2005. It was on this date that *The Today Show* aired a story titled "50 Is the New 30." On that day, Katie Couric, 48, interviewed beautifully aging supermodels Cheryl Tiegs, 58, and Christie Brinkley, 51, about new developments in the cosmetic industry. Specifically, they were breaking the news that cosmetic companies have brought older models and actresses out of retirement to appeal to aging Baby Boomers. But this wasn't the real news. Laugh lines broke out across America as Katie interrupted Christie, who was in the midst of waxing enthusiastically about Revlon's scientific breakthrough: a cosmetic product designed to reflect light out of wrinkles.

Responded Katie: "I have such mixed feelings about this. I'm so happy that people are embracing women as they age, but are they really embracing the aging process? In other words, is this about women in their 50s trying to look 30? I mean, everyone wants to look attractive, but I just wish that that didn't necessarily mean no wrinkles, you know, because I think that's a sign of experience and wisdom and the fact that you've *lived.* So do you guys ever think that not everybody has to look like they're 30 to be really beautiful?"

Cheryl Tiegs drove home Katie's point, noting that, "I don't know if we're trying to look like we're 30, I just think we're doing the best we can with our age and with what we have. I think the days of plastic surgery, pulling everything back, getting rid of every single line and wrinkle, are over."

Specialists on both women and on Baby Boomers—and especially those handful of us who are making it our business to know everything we can about marketing to the Baby Boomer woman—were beating the drums breathlessly. Commented Matt Thornhill, president of The Boomer Project, in his online newsletter: "Mark my words, America listens to Katie Couric. I bet in the next *Entertainment Weekly* we'll see that wrinkles are 'In' and botox is 'Out.'" (The jury is still out on this, by the way. But however this hot-button debate about standards of beauty in regards to aging is resolved, we can say one thing for sure: Baby Boomer women are once again hard at work expanding the range of acceptable options for themselves and the other women of their generation. Most resist being told what to do, and refuse to define aging as a problem. She demands the right to make this, and many other of her most important decisions, on an individual basis.)

From "Menopause the Musical" and laugh lines, to the growing legion of breast cancer walks, runs and related events, women have broken through the wall of shame and are openly proud of their spunky attitudes and survivorship mentality. Is it any wonder that they are approaching critical mass once again? This time they are bringing the same level of creativity, vitality, and resourcefulness to redefining their experience of life at midlife and beyond as they did to all the challenges that came before.

Advances in Healthcare

In addition to their upbeat attitudes, there are biological and technological factors that have played a role in making the "sweet spot" the demographic of choice for an increasing number of companies. Advances in nutrition, healthcare, and biotechnology have allowed this group of women to live longer and healthier than any generation of women in history. At the turn of the last century, women could expect to live on average to 48 years of age.[26] Today's woman anticipates living three or more decades of quality life beyond this. The healthcare industry, among others, has taken note, viewing her as a candidate for repeat business, new product development, and brand loyalty. These consumer appeals were essentially moot points when turning 50 meant the end of the road. They are now showing up as the marketer's key to gaining the competitive edge.

On Forging an Emotional Connection with Her

Kate Quinn,

Vice President, Marketing Strategy & Insights

WELLPOINT

Women of the Baby Boomer generation are increasingly on the healthcare industry's radar screen. Why? Because they are experiencing unprecedented health and projected longevity. They also are engaged and often responsible for making insurance and related healthcare product purchases not only for themselves, but for their families—and in the case of women-owned businesses, their employees.

One reason our industry has been slow to realize how much Boomer women influence the purchase of healthcare products and services, is that the insurance corporate cultures are strongly rooted in the male-dominated, financial realm of actuarial tables and statistical projections. In fact, until recently, with our emphasis on business-to-business sales, there hasn't been much thought paid to marketing to the ultimate consumer in general, let alone a Baby Boomer woman. This landscape is changing with the rise of the consumer-directed health plan movement. Now the consumer, who used to pay $10 a month for her health plan, may pay 70 times that amount, be it on her own or through her or her husband's employer. So, you bet she's paying attention and raising her voice!

Given that marketing to the consumer is not one of the health industry's core competencies, there have been some missteps. One tendency has been to rely on stereotypical "feminine" notions of advertising, complete with sappy, emotional language and soft-focus pastels. Again, it's one thing to appeal to the woman's feelings by telling her "we care." But if she doesn't experience that in her everyday relationship to her health insurance company, it will actually work against you. What is needed is to make that emotional connection with her through the many phases and the many roles she plays in her life, from cradle to grave. For example, instead of sending a new mother a note advising her of her disability status, send her a baby blanket, or a book on being a new parent with a letter of congratulations. This shows a new mom that we really are caring rather than just saying it.

Health is an emotional issue. By creating a positive emotional connection, one succeeds in rising above the actuarial approach. The same personal approach holds true throughout her many life stages. Today, for instance, anything that will acknowledge her challenges, making it easier on the Baby Boomer woman to care for her declining parent, will serve a similar function.

She's got a lot on her plate. In fact, anything that will help this busy woman free up time and make her life easier, overall, will trump the sentimental approach at every turn. Provide online tools that streamline her decision-making process; give her the answers to her medical questions when she needs them, 24/7; provide her with a real nurse she can actually talk to; give her the tools to research or track claims information.

Ironically, the very thing that makes this woman attractive to us—her continuing employment, her productivity, her responsibility for others—may make her a greater insurance liability risk. Why? The jury is still out on whether, given her stressed-out lifestyle, she actually will live as long as predicted. Statistically women live longer than men, but as women continue to compete, and even exceed men in terms of the pace and stress-levels of their lives, will they still continue to outlive them? Health insurance companies have a vested interest in helping women fulfill the promise of health and longevity by supporting them in their life-style behaviors and helping them and those for whom they care effectively manage their chronic illnesses. The long and short of it from a marketer's perspective: The longer women live, the more products they will have the opportunity to buy.

Kate Quinn is responsible for research across the WellPoint organization, supporting innovation, growth, strategic initiatives, and metrics. Prior to joining WellPoint, Quinn was chief marketing officer of the Group Benefits Division at The Hartford. Quinn also served as senior vice president in marketing at CIGNA Healthcare, where she was responsible for development of new products, as well as leading market research and business intelligence. Prior to CIGNA, she held executive positions in strategy, marketing, and product development in several healthcare companies.

The Impact of High-Tech

Alongside healthcare, technology is also playing a leading role in the repositioning of women 40+ as the "sweet spot" for marketers. When high-tech first made its appearance on the consumer scene, it was the young men of the Baby Boomer generation who both led and fueled the explosive growth of the industry. With its early reliance on geek-speak and programming code, rooted in fields and disciplines that had traditionally been carved out by and for men, women were late to join the party. But those days are over. While the better tech jobs are often largely the bastion of young men, awareness is rapidly growing that women of the Baby Boomer generation are increasingly the purchasers and users of the majority of consumer electronic products.

Planning to remain in the workforce for decades longer than they'd been conditioned to expect, it's as if the women of the Baby Boomer generation have been instinctively pacing themselves for the longer lifespans that are now the norm rather than the exception. Few can really justify needing to retire, as generations raised on the farm or factory floor who came before them did, simply because their physical bodies were used up. The ironic flipside of this generation's failure to save more money for their retirement years is that even if the Baby Boomer woman wanted to kick back, she can't afford the luxury of marginalization from the workplace mainstream.

As we noted earlier, as a group, they plan to remain a viable economic force well into their 70s and beyond, both spending and working. Instead of thinking retirement for her, think career change, as Baby Boomer women return to graduate and career training schools and start their own entrepreneurial endeavors in record numbers. This is a phenomenon that is not going unnoticed, as established marketers such as J. Walter Thompson are joined by a growing legion of independent branding companies who are all licking their chops over the financial clout this demographic represents.

On the Possibility of a "Boomergeddon"

The power and strength this generation of women represents should inspire marketers—and does—but it gives pause for thought, too.

As Kate Quinn of WellPoint and William Novelli, CEO of AARP, among others of our contributing authors, point out, despite the unprecedented vitality of this generation of women, the jury is still out longer-term in regard to both their physical and financial health. Some Boom-busters are going so far as to predict a "Boom-ergeddon," contending that this generation acts like it's going to dominate forever, but in reality is in a deep state of denial. A cover story in the *Los Angeles Times Magazine* featuring a critique of the generation by one of its own, University of California Professor Mike Males, asks if it is indeed possible that "holier-than-thou Baby Boomers really are just preachy, overweight, substance-abusing, criminally inclined hypocrites?"

While naysayers are provocative, the evidence suggests that given the size, problem-solving track record and monetary clout of this generation, even if the winner's circle contains less than the whole of the demographic, there is certainly still more than enough leftover to merit marketers taking a calculated risk on them. This risk can be minimized by choosing one's target consumer with care, understanding that Baby Boomers are a complex and diverse lot, spanning multiple economic strata, educational levels, and ethnicities, not to mention an 18-year age range. Beginning with Chapter Two, we will give you all the tools and intelligence you need to make wise choices about how to identify and connect with the woman who will be your best customer.

No Easy Mark

Another subject that gives the marketer pause for thought is that Boomer women engage in sophisticated decision-making processes. They know what they want and they insist on making companies accountable to them. Just as importantly, they demand being catered to, expecting marketing messages and imagery to resonate precisely with their motivations and values, with no room or tolerance for the slightest false note. To make matters even more complex, until recently Baby Boomers have been more or less in a state of rebellion and/or denial about issues related to age. Even the marketers and media who have made the attempt to serve this demographic have sometimes inadvertently alienated a substantial portion of the very market they hope to reach. Brent Green, author of *Marketing to Leading-Edge Baby Boomers,* alludes to this failure when he shares what he learned the hard way: "If you just play the 'forever young' card, you're in big trouble. Likewise, treat us only as people getting old, you've lost us again."

On the other hand, it's also not true that this generation of women can't be reached, as some marketers contend. Nor is it true that she's not worth the effort. Ford Motor Company's outreach to women in this demographic is an example of how thoughtful strategy can pave the way for connection to her.

On Recognizing Her as a Driving Force in the Marketplace

Amy Marentic,

Large Car and Crossover Product Marketing and Planning Manager

FORD MOTOR COMPANY

Ford is passionate about marketing to the Baby Boomer woman. We recognize that eight out of ten people who walk into a showroom to purchase a car are either women, or someone whose decision about which car to purchase is influenced by her. In light of this demographic's drift into the Empty Nest stage, Ford decided to revisit the notion of the family car. What would the Baby Boomer woman want to be driving at this stage of her life?

We began with an in-depth ethnographic study of her: where she lives, how she travels, how she sees herself. We uncovered a number of trends that we took into consideration when we designed a car with her needs and desires in mind: the Ford Five Hundred.

Our key finding is that she no longer needs an SUV to chauffeur her children and their friends to after-school activities—and that she can't wait to get her hands on the wheel of a sedan, once again. At the same time, however, she's not willing to give up any of the features her SUV offered. Even if she's not toting the kids around anymore, she wants enough cargo space for her occasional antiquing trips. She'd like to be able to put her mother's wheelchair in the trunk of the car and help her aging parent slide rather than step up into her passenger-side seat. She wants to feel like she's "king of the road," seated in elevated command seating. And because she's always a mother—even if her children are grown and only come to visit from time to time—the safety of her family still comes first.

For this reason, the Ford Five Hundred was built on a Volvo platform, trading on Volvo's reputation for the highest safety standards. To achieve the same features of the SUV in a sedan context, all the seats fold flat and the trunk is the biggest cargo area of any car in the United States. Finally, the Ford Five Hundred features all-wheel drive, another cue taken from the SUV.

While by no means does the Boomer woman consider herself to be old, we also tested out all of our features in Ford's "Third Age" Suit: a suit that our designers and engineers wear to simulate the restrictions of sight and movement experienced by older drivers. The Boomer woman may not need it yet for herself, but she'll appreciate such accommodations as larger gauges and adjustable pedals when her dad insists on taking the wheel.

When it came to introducing the Ford Five Hundred to the marketplace, we paid attention to the research that says that women will buy a "masculine" vehicle, but men won't buy a "feminine" one. Ironically, when we set out to please the woman, adding the features she asked for such as extra cup holders, places to store a bag or briefcase and, of course, the command seating, it appealed to the man in her life, as well. He might be thinking about transporting golf clubs, more so than his in-law's wheelchair, but by pleasing the woman in the buying equation, we get the man, as well.

To communicate effectively to her, we knew that we needed a well-trained sales force. To achieve this, we launched the biggest car training program for sales consultants in our history: 25,000 sales representatives in dozens of cities across the country. As part of the dealer training event, we shared with them key principles that work with the Baby Boomer woman: Treat her with respect, avoid hype, and tell her what she needs to know.

Amy Marentic is the product marketing and planning manager for Ford-, Lincoln-, and Mercury-branded Large Cars and Crossovers. She is responsible for the program strategy, target customer development, product content, nomenclature and pricing for several products targeting the Baby Boomer cohort. Amy holds a bachelor's degree in aerospace engineering and a master's degree in industrial and manufacturing engineering from the University of Michigan. She joined Ford in 1992 working in the aerodynamics department. She moved into the marketing and sales organization in 1999 and has held positions in product marketing, brand marketing, and sales.

A Look Ahead

The savvy marketer who takes the time to understand her and to meet her needs will find that targeting the Baby Boomer woman is well worth the effort. In the pages to come, how to navigate the complicated new terrain that she, the Baby Boomer consumer signifies, will be explored in depth. Along the way, you will be provided with:

- Insider insights about hits and misses targeting Baby Boomer women from thirty-five top marketers, including Vespa, Intel, *More* magazine, Best Western International, Logitech, Mary Kay, and more.
- The Imago Diagnostic ("ID")—A motivational assessment tool to help marketers identify what makes Baby Boomer women tick.
- Easy-to-use charts correlating the span of Baby Boomer ages to life stage and generational influences.
- Proprietary motivational research providing leading-edge intelligence to the savvy marketer seeking the competitive edge in marketing to the Baby Boomer woman.
- All the best-of-class strategies about the Baby Boomer woman that you need to make smart, competitive choices about who your customer is, what she needs to hear from you, and how to best integrate your brand into her life.

In the next chapter, we take a deeper look at Baby Boomer women in all their diversity, pointing out both the differences and commonalities between subsegments within the generation. By the time you have finished reading all seven chapters, you will have been privy to the stories of some of the most forward-thinking marketing minds in the business, and the latest research and market-tested intelligence that will help you know how she thinks, what motivates her, and how to make sure your products and services have the best chance of connecting with her.

CHAPTER TWO

She's Complex

Why There's No Such Thing as "The" Baby Boomer Woman

For starters, the Boomer generation is notable not only for its size in numbers, but also for the length of time it spans. The population tidal wave that rolled across America, as well as many other countries around the world following World War II, lasted an unprecedented 18 years. By comparison, the generation of Ikes/Silents (those born 1932 to 1945) that preceded Boomers only spans 13 years; while the generation that followed, GenX (born 1965 to 1979) clocks in at 14 years.

To get a handle on the implications of their lengthy 18-year span, it is helpful to think of the Baby Boomer generation as spread across a continuum of ages and influences, held together by a common thread of values. At one pole are what we refer to as "Leading-Edge Boomers," individuals born between 1946 and 1954, the older segment of the demographic who were entering their 60s in 2006. At the other end of the continuum are the "Trailing-Edge Boomers," born in the years between 1955 and 1964 including women still in their early 40s (see Figure 2-1).

Chronological Assumptions

The informed marketer can safely make certain broad-stroke assumptions about the motivations, needs, and interests of Leading- versus Trailing-Edge Boomers. There are, after all, certain biological and age-related realities with which even the most resourceful Baby Boomer woman will be forced to contend at a certain age or stage of her life.

The woman at 40, for instance, is more likely than a 60-year old to be juggling the demands of school-aged children who are still living at home while she is simultaneously building her career. On the other hand, the woman at 60 is likely to be more concerned with being the caretaker for her parents while dealing with the imminent financial ramifications of retirement, than is the woman in her 40s. And a woman in her late 40s and 50s, even after her facelift makes

Figure 2-1. Generational influences.[1]

	GENERATION X	TRAILING-EDGE BOOMERS	LEADING-EDGE BOOMERS	IKES/SILENTS
Born	1965-1979	1955-1964	1946-1954	1932-1945
Age in 2006	27-41	42-51	52-60	61-74
Historic/ Political	AIDS, Iran/Contra, Fall of Berlin Wall, Latchkey Kids	Vietnam, Title 9, Roe v. Wade, Nixon/Watergate	Civil Rights Movement, JFK & MLK Assassinations, Man on Moon, Vietnam	Eisenhower, McCarthyism, Korean War, Rosa Parks
Economic	Reaganomics, S&L Scandal, Stagflation	Oil embargo, Inflation, Recession	Medicare,Credit Cards, Automation in Industry	G.I. Bill, Labor Reform Act, Economic Prosperity
Social/ Trends	Aerobics Craze, Yuppies, *Saturday Night Live*, Personal Computers	Disco, Punk Rock, *Star Wars* Movie, VCRs	Elvis, The Beatles, Hippies, Woodstock, The Pill	Sinatra, *I Love Lucy*, Dr Spock, TV Dinners
Characteristics	Self-reliant, Realistic, Skeptical, Entrepreneurial	Confident, Driven Work Ethic, Status Conscious, Individualistic	Non-conformist, Seeks Personal Gratification, Idealistic	Thrifty, Conformist, Patriotic, Respects Authority
Influential Brands	Apple, Nike, Martha Stewart, Tylenol	IBM, Rolling Stone, Tab, Reebok, Dodge Caravan	McDonald's, Tupperware, Zenith, Levi's, Ms. Magazine	Burma Shave, Coca-Cola GE, Kodak, Ford

her look fifteen years younger, will still have to make decisions about how to deal with the physical challenges of menopause related to her true chronological age. Common sense dictates that it is possible to make certain age and life stage assumptions about marketing to the Baby Boomer woman. But be forewarned, this is only a preliminary step in truly understanding who she is—and how to market to her.

A major flaw in most targeted marketing campaigns is that the campaign is not "targeted" at all, but rather generalized to the point that it only reflects a stereotype about that particular segment of the population. Take the case of marketing-to-moms—the trend that took hold around the turn of the 21st century. But just who is this "Mom" that marketers are targeting? Is she only the young woman in the pastel-colored advertisement cradling her newborn? Is she the quirky "Desperate Housewife" in her 40s, chasing around two young boys after a full day at work (or her husband or the gardener in her spare time)? Could she even be the "empty nest" woman in her 50s or 60s, more engaged than she'd ever suspected in the life of her adult offspring and grandchildren? Stereotypes of motherhood aside, she, too, often continues to think of herself as "Mom." As many marketers have been finding out, there is no singular target called "moms," only a person called "Mom," in her many roles and guises.

Generational Influencers

Similarly, when marketers talk about targeting the Baby Boomer woman, are they only thinking about the long-married female, entrenched in her relationships and ways of being in the world? Or are they also thinking of the possibility of a widow, "single and loving it," a self-chosen divorcee, or even a blushing bride? Once we leave the relatively safe perch of biological markers, marketers are on fresh, new, and largely unexplored demographic terrain. The fact is that age and even physical milestones are not the most reliable indicators of either her needs, or what it is that makes her tick. To continue the process of getting to know her in all her glorious complexity, we must turn next to understanding her generational influencers.

Every generation holds beliefs and ideals that were shaped by the key historic, social, economic, and political events of their formative years. A unique convergence of core influences shapes each generation as a distinct demographic in its own right, with its own special tone and flavor.

Some of the key qualities and characteristics at the heart of the Baby Boomer generation, pertaining to both men and women, are an orientation towards idealism, a preference for individualism, and a tendency towards immediate gratification. Figure 2-1 summarizes differing influences and characteristics acting upon the generations in the United States. These influencers are critically important for the marketer to take into consideration when strategizing about product and services attributes, marketing messages, and approaches.

Referring back to Figure 2-1, you can better pinpoint the relevant emotional tenor that will appeal to your target demographic. If you want your product or service to attract positive attention from a Leading-Edge Boomer, for instance, consider marketing messages that appeal to her desire for nonconformity and idealism. Ameriprise Financial has done an excellent job targeting the Leading-Edge woman, both in print and television ads. One multipage magazine ad is titled: "A generation as unique as this needs a new generation of personal financial planning." The graphic surrounding the headline is a composite of nostalgic photos from the 50s and 60s. Among the most prominent photographs are iconic images holding special appeal for her. This woman's mom—the woman of the 1950s, wearing classic pearls and Jacqueline Kennedy hairdo—is fading into polka dots, while a flower child playing the flute comes into full-color focus. A lava lamp, psychedelic Love poster, and an African-American woman with a stylish Afro, address her ongoing history of nonconformity. Appealing to her idealism, is a strategically positioned black and white photograph of a space capsule that one assumes is on its way to the moon. Ameriprise concludes its pitch by offering, "to help you get to *what's next* in your life."

On Appealing to Her Values

Joanne Sachse Mogren,

Vice President of Merchandising/Apparel Division

GARNET HILL

The experiences, events and cultural revolution of the 1960s and 1970s had a dramatic effect on the Baby Boomer generation's perception of the world; they emerged with a much more dynamic relationship to global events, they had the confidence to challenge authority, and saw that they had the power to effect change. They embraced the concepts of individuality and creativity, and rallied against excess; they were turned on by music, art, and politics that celebrated peace and love and a better world. Their experiences gave them very different expectations for their futures, and for their roles and responsibilities in the world. They engaged actively in the workplace and achieved much greater autonomy in choosing lifestyles that expressed their individual choices. They were passionate about enhancing the quality of their lives.

At Garnet Hill, we are passionate about providing great product offerings that bring both aesthetic and practical fulfillment to people's lives. There are many elements of our brand and lifestyle approach that create a natural affinity to Baby Boomer women. For instance, we design with an eye to beauty and creativity first, balanced by comfort and practicality. It is rooted in the quality of natural fibers, supported by original artwork and executed with attention to detail. Casual and classic, it appeals to a broad age range. It is a tasteful product with a twist that makes you feel good when you wear it. Inspired by the colors, textures and diversity of our worldwide travel as well as our immediate surroundings, it has its own point of view.

We support our merchandise with simple, yet sophisticated, creative presentations that also illustrate our commitment to aesthetics as well as quality. Our models have an attainable, friendly beauty and positive energy. They are styled and accessorized in unexpected, interesting ways. Our copy is intelligent and informative. These are very critical elements in clarifying and enhancing our brand.

Baby Boomer women understand and relate to the values and lifestyle that our product and presentation convey. This may be in part because Garnet Hill's original culture emerged as a result of the values of that generation. The catalog still represents and celebrates many of those aspirations—individuality, creativity, intelligence, comfort, quality, fulfillment, and simplicity. It comes across as a special and carefully edited collection. Although not inexpensive, our merchandise is perceived as having fair and lasting value for its price. Our customers appreciate the uniqueness and exclusivity of our product and view it as another way to express their individuality. The appeal is not about a particular age, but about creative, lifestyle-enhancing choices that transcend age.

Joanne Sachse Mogren is vice president of apparel merchandising at Garnet Hill, Inc., a 29-year-old direct mail order catalog specializing in natural fiber apparel and home furnishings, in Franconia, New Hampshire. She joined Garnet Hill in 1982, and currently oversees the merchandising, design and product development for both *Garnet Hill* and *Growing Up with Garnet Hill*, their spin-off children's title.

An Overlay of Status

For a Trailing-Edge Boomer, idealism is still the ticket. However, for her, the emphasis shifts subtly from non-conformity to individualism, with an overlay of status consciousness thrown in for good measure. Napa Auto Care Center gets it right for her with an ad that is summarized by the tagline: "Get the Good Life." The print ad for the auto care company features a typical Trailing-Edge mom's spontaneous hodgepodge of magnets and personal messages scattered over the front of her high-end stainless steel refrigerator. The overriding vision is one of a mom who is giving her all to parenting at its finest. But this woman is not only living up to the ideals of her generation, but raises them. For in addition to the trendy refrigerator that confers status upon her, she has obviously won bragging rights through the endless activities with which she has involved her children: swim lessons, dance class, baseball practice, and piano lessons, among them.

And don't feel that you've got to show a man walking on the moon or hit every generational bell and whistle to connect with her. In fact, if the nostalgic card is played too blatantly, it can come across as gratuitous. She will have her antennae up for any note that resonates as disingenuous.

On Getting Nostalgia Right

Cindy Marshall,

Director of Marketing

THE VERMONT COUNTRY STORE

As "purveyors of the practical and hard to find," The Vermont Country Store brings back forgotten items that hold memories of days past. After conducting studies, we identified that we have two core groups of customers: WWII/ Depression Era and Baby Boomer cohorts. However, we found that the approach we take in our core catalog, using black and white illustrations and imagery and no-frill layouts, didn't connect with our growing Baby Boomer segment. Armed with this knowledge, we set out to market to this customer segment differently than the older cohort. We launched a color catalog and wrote unique copy aiming to "speak" to them more relevantly. Great idea, but this approach wasn't enough for savvy Boomers. There was no overt indication that we were introducing something new and particularly relevant to them.

Since then, we have applied our knowledge to getting it right for Boomers, and Boomer women in particular. We've focused on a product assortment that is more relevant to this younger demographic, and in particular, the Leading-Edge Boomers. Products like Tangee Lipstick, Lanz Tyrolean flannel nightgowns, and Caroler Candles strike a chord. We don't present them with the more practical products geared toward senior living because they don't want to be reminded of the health implications of aging. And they certainly don't feel the need to be *too* prepared for that stage of life.

This midlife nostalgic consumer doesn't need more stuff; she needs more meaning in her life. We speak to Boomer women by offering emotional relevance. Our products both trigger and satisfy emotional responses and the desire to relive memorable times. Family, health, and philanthropy drive her priorities—and we speak to that. The Vermont Country Store helps make family connections by giving her the opportunity to gift or "hand down" traditions that may have long ago been sold in a yard sale. It's not uncommon to hear customers say, "This was my favorite toy as a child. I want to give it to my grandson."

Cindy Marshall has over twenty years of traditional direct marketing experience. Currently, she serves as director of marketing for The Vermont Country Store where she is responsible for catalog and e-commerce marketing efforts. Previously, Cindy was vice president of marketing for Ross-Simons and vice president of marketing at eZiba.com. Cindy also enjoyed four years at L.L. Bean where she was part of the management team that launched Freeport Studio, a women's apparel brand targeted to Boomer women. Additionally, Cindy held the position of L.L. Bean Visa Loyalty marketing manager. Her extensive background also includes senior management positions at J.Jill, Appleseed's, and *Inc.* magazine.

Promise and Peril of Nostalgia

Some companies who have used iconic songs from the 60s or 70s to sell their products or services can attest to this first-hand: Baby Boomer women have been known to express outrage at what they think of as the too-conspicuously obvious manipulation of their emotions. While it is true, for example, that some Boomers (probably more men than women) enjoyed seeing Bob Dylan hawking women's lingerie, there were other Boomers (probably more women than men) who felt that putting Dylan in an overtly commercial context, particularly one that could be seen as objectifying women as sexual objects, was degrading and even sacrilegious. While nostalgia generally appeals to her, the Baby Boomer woman wants her roots and memories honored—not exploited. Unless nostalgia is well done, stereotypical references to the peace and love generation, and the like, will only make the Boomer woman feel misunderstood, and even angry.

An alternative, with less downside risk, is to let your message be informed by her values. An example of this is Olay's, "Love the skin you're in™" campaign. In one striking magazine ad for an anti-aging, anti-blemish moisturizer, the headline reads: "Wrinkles and pimples. What's next, bifocals and ripped jeans?" The photo shows an attractive 40- or perhaps even 50-something woman, laugh lines having evaded the art director's touch-up pen, peering over her hip reading glasses and looking very at-home in embroidered jeans with obvious holes at the knees. The frayed jeans are not only items of nostalgia from her distant past, but also something she is very likely to be wearing today, as well as tomorrow for that matter. The embroidered symbols on her jeans, hand-crocheted flowers in the style popular in the 1960s, are a subtle and perhaps even subconscious appeal to the iconography of her own history.

But subtleties aside, the ad consciously and effectively delivers not only a message but a product that is relevant to her current needs, desires, and experiences. It communicates while respecting her core values, encompassing both individualism and nonconformity with the icing on the cake: a large serving of self-acceptance. (More on the psychosocial motivators for the Baby Boomer will be shared in Chapter Four, when this ad will be revisited as an example of a Stage Three "Aspirational Boomer" motivational archetype.)

Retailers Who Get Her

Tending more often than not to get it right are the specialty retailers offering apparel for Baby Boomer women. Companies such as J.Jill, Appleseed's, Coldwater Creek, Garnet Hill, and Canada's Yzza build their consumers' values into the very fabric of the garments they sell. *How does it feel against her skin? Can it be washed instead of dry-cleaned? Is it possible to be both stylish and comfortable?* Later in this book, contributing authors representing a number of these companies, revisit the importance of these and similar questions, highlighting the overriding importance of paying attention to her core values. For example, Cindy Marshall, who before joining The Vermont Country Store helped pioneer the Baby Boomer woman's apparel marketplace comments, "As a Boomer myself, I shop at places that offer me unique but multifunctional pieces that tie together items I've collected at boutiques, catalogs, and even discount retailers. I'm not as concerned about where I bought it as I am about how it fits into my definition of being an independent, feminine professional."

When it comes to core values, it is important to note that in many ways, Leading-Edge and Trailing-Edge Boomers have more in common with one another than they do with the women of either the Ikes/Silents or Gen X. But differentiating the Baby Boomer woman from the general population of women is only one more stop along the way to truly understanding what she wants and how to market to her.

Gender Differences

Pausing briefly to catch our breath, we are about to forge ahead to the next complicating factor. For not only does the Baby Boomer woman differ from the women of other generations, but she also differs from the men of her own let alone other generations.

On the Difference Between Marketing to Men and to Women

Caleb Mason,

Director of Corporate Marketing

DELORME

Having worked for a company that markets heavily to women (Konica) and one that markets heavily to men (DeLorme), I've figured out the essential difference: *Men are more interested in how things work than in actual benefits/outcomes. Women are interested in benefits and resent the amount of time men have to waste in understanding how things work!*

The differences first became obvious to me in the mid-1990s, observing men and women in focus groups discussing the new digital cameras. The men wanted to know how the pictures were captured, what kind of CMOS (Complimentary Metal Oxide Semiconductor) chipset was included. The women really only became interested when they began to brainstorm how easy sharing pictures over the Web might be. The men . . . sharing? You must be joking.

Caleb Mason is director of corporate marketing for the leading digital mapping and GPS innovator. After serving at Little, Brown and as VP/associate publisher at publishing start-up Salem House, he joined Konica. At Konica, Caleb was instrumental in launching new digital imaging products and services, including the world's first large-scale consumer online photo service.

Another Word About the Differences Between Men and Women

Simply put, men and women are wired differently. He prefers the big picture and broad strokes, using a more linear and logical approach to making decisions. Her decision-making process, on the other hand, takes a layered and cyclical path, where subtlety, details, research, and word-of-mouth play influential roles. Marketers who have championed the marketing-to-woman trend referred to in Chapter One have, by now, teased out virtually every nuance regarding the differences between the purchasing styles and patterns of men and women in general. We will resist the temptation to recreate the entire body of knowledge that is readily accessed through such texts as *Don't Think Pink: What Really Makes Women Buy—and How to Increase Your Share of This Crucial Market* by Lisa Johnson and Andrea Learned, and *Marketing to Women: How to Understand, Reach, and Increase Your Share of the World's Largest Market Segment* by Martha Barletta. (For a more comprehensive list of gender and generational resources, see the Resources section at the back of the book.) In Chapter Five, however, we will take a deeper dive into the differences between men and women as it pertains, more particularly, to the Baby Boomer generation. At that time, we, along with a number of our contributing authors, will give the marketer specific guidance on how to capitalize on her unique purchasing behaviors and characteristics.

The important thing to keep in mind at this juncture is the level of sophistication regarding gender marketing that is necessary to connect effectively with her. In other words, as Fran Philip of L.L. Bean warns, resist the urge to "just shrink it and pink it," and you're part way there.

On Why Not to Just Shrink it and Pink it

Fran Philip,
Chief Merchandising Officer

L.L. BEAN

Over the past decade, women in their mid-forties and older have emerged as a powerful consumer: influential, smart, and savvy. Despite this, the Baby Boomer woman remains very underserved in the market, and to some degree annoyed about it. L.L. Bean, as a leading multichannel merchant of casual and active clothing and outdoor equipment, views her as a formidable opportunity and feels she deserves a lot of respect. Seventy percent of our customers are women, most are 45 to 55 years old, college-educated, with grown children and a career. These women are likely also driving the decision-making process on what the other 30 percent of our customers are purchasing.

The Baby Boomer woman, more than any generation before her, knows her own power and doesn't want to be taken lightly or marketed to in a disingenuous way. She's too experienced for that. She's a price-conscious shopper, not because she isn't well-off, but because she's smart and looking for value. We know she's multitasking and has a very complex, time-starved life. So, as a brand, we ask: How do we solve problems for her? How do we make things more convenient for her? How do we make life easier for her? Whether we're thinking about a marketing campaign, a catalog layout, or the thought process that goes into the development of a specific product, it's all about building those qualities into the experience: the problem-solving, the practical, the functional, the comfortable, and the convenience.

One of our biggest growth areas right now is in developing sporting equipment specifically for her. This doesn't mean just taking a man's backpack, cutting it down in size and offering it in more feminine colors—what's known in the industry as "shrink it and pink it." L.L. Bean has made a commitment not to take that approach. For example, we created a new pack about a year ago called the Celia Day Pack. Our development team worked extensively with product and field testers to try out all the women's packs currently on the market. They highlighted what features they liked and eliminated what they did not like. Then we mixed and matched all these features and built a totally new pack from the ground up. It's got everything she wants: it's proportioned for her frame, is adjustable (because women come in lots of different sizes), and it comes in a variety of colors. The pack was an immediate success. This first women's-only pack became our best-selling product of all the backpacks we offer, including men's.

We did the same thing for a kayak we're introducing in spring called the Calypso kayak. The number one thing women told us they worry about in a kayak is weight. They want to be able to carry it and put it on top of their car by themselves. Fiberglass kayaks are extremely lightweight, but also fragile and expensive. We found a material both lightweight and durable, at her price-point. Also, the shape and size of the seat and cockpit are proportioned for a woman's body instead of a man's.

L.L. Bean strives to build a lot of integrity into our products from the ground up, specifically for the 50-year-old female Baby Boomer. Whether it's daypacks, kayaks, snowshoes, luggage, active wear, or casual apparel, if all you're doing is addressing superficialities, she'll find you out. Get the product attributes and pricing right for her first—and then you can worry about whether to make it robin's egg blue, neon green, or yes, even pink.

Fran Philip, before assuming her current position, served as senior vice president/general manager for two of L.L. Bean's seven strategic business units: L.L. Bean Home and Freeport Studio. During her tenure, the Home Division has been one of the fastest growing and most profitable divisions of L.L. Bean. Before coming to L.L. Bean, Fran was one of the original founders of Calyx & Corolla, an innovative direct mail concept specializing in fresh flowers shipped directly to the consumer from the grower via Federal Express. Prior to Calyx & Corolla, Fran held positions at Williams-Sonoma, the Nature Company, and the Gap.

Cultural Differences

Adding yet another layer of complexity, we turn to the fact that out of the 78 million Boomers living in the United States, one in three belongs to a racial or ethnic minority. These include 9.1 million African Americans, 8 million Hispanics, 3 million Asians, and 6 million who are multiracial.[2] African-American, Hispanic, and Asian-American cultures are not homogenous, and neither are the Baby Boomer women of these cultures. They will tune out messages that fail to recognize the values, vocabulary, and insider humor that exist in their distinct cultural markets. Pepper Miller shares her intelligence with us regarding her particular area of expertise on this important point.

On Marketing to Distinctions

Pepper Miller,
President
THE HUNTER-MILLER GROUP

African-American Boomer females represent a powerful, desirable, and distinctive consumer group. Not only do Black females overall control $403 billion in buying power, but they also are the means for reaching the Black market in general. The appropriate marketing investments must be made, and relevant messages must be created, that celebrate their decision-making power, individuality, style, and success.

This call for relevance to this distinctive consumer is a departure from the mindset in marketing today that focuses on appealing to lifestyle similarities among various demographic segments. Rather than develop relevant communications targeted toward individual groups, the theory is that this "multicultural" approach will appeal to all audiences across the board.

Recognizing the key cultural differences between African-American women and their White female counterparts makes all the difference in determining whether marketing programs and communications are relevant to African-American women. African-American females are on average educated, motivated, and visible in all aspects of society. Whether single or married, Black females are even more likely than White females to control the purse strings in their households. Furthermore, African-American women have always pushed the envelope of fashion trends and have made a tremendous impact on hairstyles and hair color. As a result, they continue to reject the general market beauty standards and embrace their own style and body image. This behavior has motivated the fashion and marketing industries to take heed, learn, and incorporate these ideas into their product lines and marketing plans.

The 2005 Window on Our Women study (WOWII), the first ever segmentation study on African-American women commissioned by *Essence* magazine and conducted independently by Lieberman Research Worldwide and The Hunter-Miller Group, details how Black women are a distinctive and desirable segment in the areas of fashion, media, retailing, and finance. While the study encompasses findings from Black women age 18 to 64, for purposes of this book the following findings are specific to comparing African-American female Boomers to their Caucasian female Boomer counterparts.

Among the findings:

- Black female Boomers are more likely than White female Boomers to be the primary decision makers for their household's travel, home electronics, financial services and investments, insurance, automobile, and real estate purchases.

- When surveyed about career and education decisions, more African-American females than their White counterparts believe that they must do work they enjoy in order to be successful. In addition, Black women are more likely than White females to say that they have overcome barriers and obstacles in their life, and indicate that they have more confidence in themselves and in their physical appearance. Thus, self-reliance is important to African-American women as 53 percent deem they must manage their responsibilities with peace of mind in order to be successful, as compared to 40 percent of White females.

* Lastly, compared to White females, Black females are four times more likely to see cultural heritage as a benchmark for success. Thus, 53 percent of African-American women feel they must stay true to their cultural heritage in order to be successful, as compared to 13 percent of White females.

* These Black women are readily reached using targeted media and through grassroots efforts in churches, Black organizations, and the community. Black women use general market media, but they embrace Black media. For example, of Black women who rely on magazines as a source of information, 70 percent rely solely on African-American magazines, while only 5 percent rely on general market magazines.

Marketers hoping to reach and sell to African-American women need to note their differences from White females and, therefore, target and service these women differently.

Pepper Miller is coauthor of *What's Black About It? Insights to Increase Your Share of the Changing African-American Market* (Paramount Market Publishing, www.paramountbooks.com). She is president of The Hunter-Miller Group, Inc., a Chicago-based market research and planning firm that helps Fortune 500 companies understand and effectively market their products and services to African-American consumers.

Pharmaceutical giant GlaxoSmithKline is an example of a company that is doing a good job targeting the Baby Boomer woman, with a specific promotional outreach to the African-American Boomer woman. To promote their calcium supplement, Os-Cal, they hosted a series of Os-Cal Chewable "We Matter, Vitamin D Matters!" forums at churches across the country. The forums are education events, targeted to teaching this demographic the importance of maintaining both bone health—and inner spiritual beauty. The forums were launched with a Washington, D.C. inauguration held in conjunction with the National Urban League's annual conference and featured Oprah's *O* magazine's "Dream Team of Health Experts"—Byllye Avery, Dr. Janet Taylor, and Dr. Susan Taylor. The convergence of public service and marketing addresses a real concern: While 70 percent of all women age 51 to 70 and nearly 90 percent of women older than 70 aren't getting enough vitamin D, African-American women are at even greater risk. African-American women between age 19 and 49 have ten times less vitamin D in their blood than their Caucasian counterparts.[3]

Isabel Valdés, Hispanic marketing expert, discusses unique marketing challenges and opportunities inherent in the Hispanic marketplace.

On Marketing to Hispanic Baby Boomer Women

Isabel Valdés,

President

ISABEL VALDÉS CONSULTING, ***IVC***

The Hispanic/Latino population, having ballooned from 6.9 million in 1960 to 35.3 million in 2000 has grown faster than any other "cultural" or ethnic group in U.S. history. (Note that the 2000 figure does not include 4 million Puerto Ricans and the estimated U.S. Census undercount.)

One of the biggest differences between Caucasian and Hispanic Boomers in the United States is that the vast majority of Hispanics of this generation were born outside the United States. They emigrated from Mexico, Central and South America, Cuba, and Puerto Rico. They spent their core formative years in the traditional culture of their country of origin, that is to say, "Hispanic." On average, they have lived in the United States about half of their lives, unlike younger Hispanic generations who, having lived from childhood in the United States, have more fully assimilated into mainstream American culture and lifestyle.

Hispanic Boomers are usually caught between two cultures. And being older does increase the challenge to integrate into American systems and lifestyle. For instance, though the "empty nest" phenomenon is challenging and emotionally charged for many Boomer moms, it is doubly difficult for the Hispanic mom. Unlike their Anglo-American counterpart, who probably left home for college right after high school, Boomer Hispanic women were not so independent, remaining at home until marriage. Lacking a similar experience of their own, it is harder to reconcile their children's—especially their daughters'—departure into the world. In fact, in some instances, Hispanic daughters are discouraged to go away to college by their families because it breaks with the traditional model of living with the parents, not by themselves.

Latino Boomer women tend to put family above all else, sacrificing in the extreme for their husbands, kids, parents and extended relations. This Hispanic woman will respond to messaging, services, and products that speak to her sense of duty to keep family bonds strong.

Not surprisingly, Latino Boomers are very involved with their grandchildren and aging parents. For Hispanic Boomer women, it is a given that *every* vacation, as long as her parents and in-laws are alive, involves multiple generations. Many juggle the logistics of caring for aging parents who in many cases still live outside the United States. How to fulfill that inner craving of being all together? "In-Culture" marketing can understand and address their needs. For example, Princess Cruises has tailored their accommodations and programs for this multigenerational family group. Additionally, they offer cruises that start and end at ports in Mexico and South America, allowing parents of Hispanic-American Boomers to more easily join in on the vacation.

This strong emotional pull of intergenerational family bonds in Latino culture has deep implications for consumer product marketing as well. For example, Johnson & Johnson, when developing a new diabetes test kit, took into consideration that Hispanics tend to over-index with diabetes. Instead of positioning their Latino product message as "do this for yourself," the marketing campaign communicated "address your health issues so you can be there and enjoy your kids *and* grandkids." Appealing to this Latino deep emotional bond, sense of duty, and commitment to family legacy was a successful way to capture the attention of this valuable and growing consumer segment.

Isabel Valdés, a pioneer in Hispanic marketing and founder of "In-Culture Marketing,™" heads Isabel Valdés Consulting, an In-Culture marketing consulting firm. Her extensive client list includes Fortune 100 and 1000 companies, nonprofit organizations and government. Ms. Valdés released her third book in late 2002, *Marketing to American Latinos, A Guide to the In-Culture Approach*, Part II (PMP, Ithaca, N.Y.). Presently she is working on a new book and sits on several boards, including Pepsi Co/Frito-Lay's Hispanic advisory board, Scholastic, National Council La Raza, and the Latino Community Foundation. She is a frequent guest lecturer and public speaker in the United States and abroad.

No marketing specialty firm can be an expert in all ethnicities, religions, genders, cultures, and generations. There is, in fact, growing recognition among marketers of the importance of insider expertise, coupled with an equally large and humble respect for any particular niche-specialist's limitations. There are early indications of a trend toward the formations of alliances between cultural, gender, and generational experts, collaborating on marketing initiatives targeted specifically to meet this demand for increasingly sophisticated market segmentation.

Economic Considerations

There is one more differentiator to be at least briefly addressed before leaving this chapter: her economic status. Marketers of many products and services require their prospective consumer to have attained a certain level of affluence. Be it a luxury cruise or a top-of-the-line refrigerator, Baby Boomer or not, the reality is, in the words of *More* magazine: "Our product is quite simply not for everybody."

The sophisticated marketer, regardless of who the target market is, will want to know that there's at least a minimal correlation between the cost of the offering and the financial resources of the consumer. But keep in mind that there are more contributing factors than simply the money in her bank account that makes one segment of the Baby Boomer woman population a more desirable target than another.

More magazine educates advertisers about sub-segments within the Baby Boomer woman demographic, placing her financial status within an attitudinal context. In their recent *Age of Mastery* study of Boomer women, *More* revealed that those women with a higher average household income are not necessarily the most financially optimistic, nor inclined to value quality more than price. In other words, motivation and need can override household income when it comes to her purchase decisions.

Along with gender, generational, and ethnic considerations, understanding her life stage drivers plays a critical role in making your product or service connect with her current life challenges. In Chapter Three we focus on the inherent opportunities for marketers as Baby Boomer women move through the complexity of various life stages.

CHAPTER THREE

She's Her Stage, Not Her Age

Leveraging Her Life Transitions

Ask a woman over 40 whether she identifies with her age, and most likely you'll find a genuine disconnect between the date on her driver's license and how she's looking, acting, and feeling. Nowhere was this discrepancy between expectation and reality more obvious than on January 1, 2006, when the first of the Leading-Edge Baby Boomers began turning 60. Based on our study of 100 women's attitudes about aging, we decided that the time was ripe to call for an "Adjust Your Chronological Clock Day."[1]

This tongue-in-cheek chronological corrective suggests that women 40+ should feel entitled to set their age clock back ten years to more accurately reflect their real sense of themselves, as well as to give marketers a more precise read of their "true" age. Rather than market to her B.C. "*Birth Certificate*" age, we suggested that marketers think in terms of her A.C. "*Adjusted Chronological*" age. Enthusiastic response to this notion poured in from around the world, with women throwing in with the chronological adjustment notion from as far away as Australia and Ireland.

It is not only Baby Boomers who don't feel their age. "Twixters"—twenty-somethings—are delaying serious career choices and marriage into their 30s and 40s, years later than their parents, the Leading-Edge Boomers, began settling down. It is as if across the board, the generations are organically adjusting to their extended lifespans, in many cases negotiating life stages and issues years later than previous generations. This is a seismic multigenerational shift, impacting marketing initiatives that can no longer rely on traditional age segmentation to reflect any demographic's true motivations, interests, or needs.

Life Stage Marketing

If the Baby Boomer woman doesn't resonate with the age on her driver's license, then with what does she identify? The same study that inspired "Adjust Your Chronological Clock Day" found that not only did the women *not* identify with their ages, but they didn't identify with the whole notion of "aging." None of the women in our study identified themselves as senior citizens, elderly, or aged. Rather, they defined themselves by the issues and opportunities they were facing at the time. For example, one woman who had decided to go back to school to get her advanced degree identified herself primarily as a "student." Others identified themselves as being at "the peak of their careers." Some were "golfers" or "social activists" and rarely, even when they were no longer working, did they self-identify as "retirees." Some continued to define themselves in terms relating to the needs and concerns of their immediate family. They were caretakers to declining husbands or parents, grandparents, or surprisingly, still "mom" to their (technically) adult son or daughter.

Through it all, they were viewing the issues and opportunities of midlife and beyond through the same lens that has always captured this generation of women's attention: How to find meaning, be productive, reduce stress, make a contribution to society, and relish the fully lived life.

Their aversion to thinking in terms of "the challenge of aging" was not denial that new, and often problematic, things were happening to them and that biological age was a contributing factor. Rather, the majority preferred to define themselves by the problem-solving attitudes and aspirations they were bringing to bear against the occasions to which they were arising.

Appealing to the Baby Boomer woman on the basis of her life circumstances, rather than defining her by age, is what marketers refer to as *life stage marketing*. Every one of this woman's new life stages generates a period of redefinition, transition, and a series of new experiences to negotiate. This, in turn, provides opportunities for the savvy marketer to help these women problem-solve their way forward, aspiring to make the best of whatever life brings their way.

On Playing Financial Catch Up

Lisa Caputo,

President and CEO, Women & Co., and

Chief Marketing, Advertising, and Community Relations Officer,

Global Consumer Group

CITIGROUP

In 2000, Citigroup recognized that there was a true need—not just a marketing niche—to create a financial service dedicated to women. The market for our specialized offerings includes Baby Boomer women, who represent a substantial part of our membership. Although Baby Boomer women have made enormous economic strides, we have found that they need and want more knowledge about how to build wealth and leverage financial resources based on their unique life stage needs. Each transition point in life calls for a new set of information, and it's almost impossible for women to be fully armed to navigate each twist and turn. Our members include women from all walks of life—professional women; stay-at-home moms; divorced, widowed, single, and married women. The unifying factor is that these women want to learn how to be more active participants in planning their and their family's financial future.

In order to reach Baby Boomer women, our strategy has been to break through the clutter of traditional financial advertising to speak to the real concerns in a tone that is unapologetically feminine, confident, and inspiring.

Below are some of our findings of particular interest to Baby Boomer women:

- Women live longer and run the risk of outliving retirement savings. Being closer to retirement age than younger women, Boomer women have a shorter time horizon to play "financial catch up" and ensure they have enough income to last them through their retirement years.
- Many Boomer women are "sandwiched" financially and emotionally, providing monetary and other support for minor or adult children, as well as aging relatives.
- One-third of women who become widowed are younger than age 60 (Women's Institute for a Secure Retirement). As such, Boomer women are more likely to face the financial challenges of widowhood and to be in the position of the sole financial decision maker.

Our current print ads cross-leverage familiar concerns and imagery of health and beauty, as well as use humor to empower women to take care of their finances. Usually, magazine ads attempt to convince women to spend their money. Our ads highlight the alternative—where a woman can turn when she wants to learn about saving and investing her money.

The feedback has been outstanding. Women are responding because we are striking the right balance of humor, information, and respect.

Lisa Caputo assumed her current role, in October 2005, as chief marketing, advertising, and community relations officer, Global Consumer Group, and executive director of Citigroup Brand Management Committee. Additionally, Lisa created and oversees (since January 2000) Women and Company, a membership program that provides a host of solutions to address the distinct financial needs of women. Women and Company members account for over $13 billion in assets at Citigroup. Prior to joining Citigroup, Lisa was with the Walt Disney Company and the CBS Corporation. Before embarking on her business career, Lisa served as press secretary to Hillary Rodham Clinton for four years.

Here are three key takeaways for marketers from Figure 3-1.

1. *Within the Baby Boomer generation, life-stage events are not age specific.*

The woman in her mid-40s may be taking care of an elderly parent, and so may the woman in her mid-60s or even, given the fact of our unprecedented longevity, the woman in her 70s. Regardless of her age, she will share certain concerns with other caregiving women in the same circumstance. Similarly, a woman in her late 40s who is a grandmother may exhibit consumption patterns regarding gift purchases that are more similar to those of a woman in her 60s

Figure 3-1. Female life stage constellation.

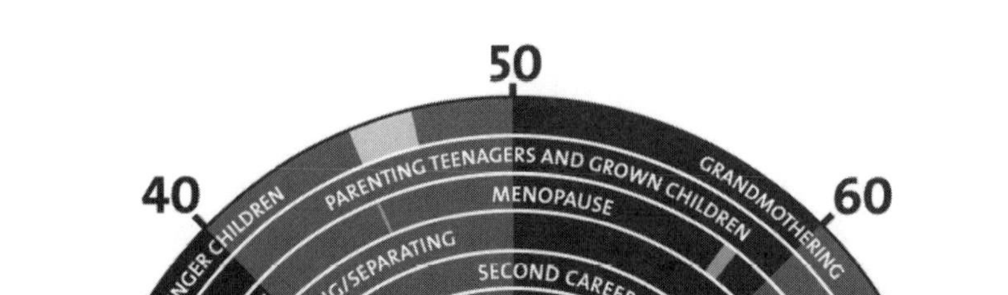

who also has grandchildren, than to those of a woman in her 40s who doesn't have children.

2. *As an individual, she is in multiple life stages simultaneously.*

Financial advisers and institutions please note: She may still be paying off her children's school loans while applying for new school loans for herself. Along the same lines, she may be an empty-nester, grandparent, and dating—all at the same time.

3. *She is likely to revisit a number of life stages multiple times.*

There is the tendency to think of the Baby Boomer woman's negotiation of life stages as linear and consecutive. But there is the distinct possibility, for example, that she will be caring for an elderly parent more than once in her life. Between her own parents and in-laws, as well as multiple spouses of divorced and remarried parents, she may be deemed caretaker four or even more times. And the marketer who thinks that the Baby Boomer woman is likely to have her "midlife crisis" in her 40s or 50s (as was proposed by a much-discussed *Newsweek* magazine cover in 2005), will be taken utterly by surprise when many of these women circle around and renegotiate their lives in identity crisis mode yet again—in their 60s or even 70s.

On Marketing to All Her Life Stages

William D. Novelli,
Chief Executive Officer

AARP

In 2005, AARP signed on its ten millionth Baby Boomer—with the greatest area of membership growth being women 50 to 59 years old. We're making progress attracting Boomer women to our ranks—but our success is mixed, since retention of these Boomers is not as high as we'd like. We're finding that one key to keeping Boomers engaged is making sure that we have products and services geared to their specific needs. For instance, we recognize that many Boomer women are going back to school at the same time they are still paying for their children's education. A financial product that makes it easy for them to borrow money to pay for their own schooling, too, is something that we're putting together. Others may be interested in motorcycle insurance, an offering they might not have expected to see from AARP, but that is already among our products.

Whatever it is that we offer, we've got to take into consideration this generation's demand for instant gratification. In marketing terms, we refer to this as "speed to value." If a

Boomer sends us her $12.50, she doesn't want to wait six weeks to get her first copy of our magazine from us. She may cringe that she's old enough for AARP. But if she can use her membership card fast, and get real value for it, she'll say, "Hey, thanks."

We hear a lot about the long lifespans for women of the Baby Boomer generation. These extra years will provide many opportunities for marketers who have products and services that will address her various life stage needs and opportunities. But longevity is a double-edged sword for her. Not only is she living longer, but so are her parents and grandparents.

Take the case of caregiving, for example, one of the most powerful forces impacting the Boomer woman over the coming years. Known as part of "the sandwich generation," she's really more of a "club sandwich" these days, with spending a disproportionate amount of time dealing with the needs of not only her adult children and aging parents, but her grandparents as well. The business community is waking up to the fact that at 50-something, the Boomer woman is often juggling a full-time job while searching for assisted living for the older generations, dealing with their finances, physicians, living arrangements and more. Companies are thinking about how they can help her with this burden. At the White House Conference on Aging, AARP co-sponsored an exhibit addressing how technology can be of assistance. One product getting attention is a monitor located in her own home or office that allows her to keep tabs on her parents who may be living alone in another geographical area.

Caregiving is something that concerns the 50-year old now. But the real story about Baby Boomers is not just that they're turning 50 or 60, but how soon it will be that they are going to be turning 80 and 90. And are they prepared? The days are over when one could say that she would just live on her social security check. And research suggests that this generation is comprised of poor savers, with a substantial percentage of them not only unable to put savings away for the future, but still accumulating debt. Many are going to outlive their husbands and their savings, with the likelihood that there is going to be a broad-scale downscaling in terms of their economic status. As the picture becomes clearer to her, her level of financial literacy is rapidly expanding. There is a huge market opportunity in developing financial services and products, such as annuities and 401(k)-type offerings, designed especially for her needs.

There are health issues, as well. Certainly, there are some Baby Boomers who could run a marathon tomorrow. AARP studies show that 60 percent don't get enough exercise. Obesity is threatening to reverse much of the longevity gains made in the last few years.

The Western, industrialized world can afford to address the challenges of a society that is growing older. The question is, will it? These are issues that call for activism—an arena that has traditionally skewed male. AARP views Baby Boomer women, with their higher educations and heightening motivation, as a potential pool of activists, on the verge of getting involved politically, economically, and socially. The message has got to be communicated that by working together to fulfill the promise that longevity offers, the larger society will benefit, as well.

William D. Novelli is chief executive officer of AARP, a membership organization of 36 million people age 50 and older. He joined AARP in January 2000 as associate executive director and became CEO in June 2001. Prior to joining AARP, Mr. Novelli was president of the Campaign for Tobacco-Free Kids and executive vice president of CARE, the world's largest private relief and development organization. Mr. Novelli cofounded and was president of Porter Novelli, an international marketing/public relations agency founded to apply marketing to social and health issues. He retired from the firm in 1990 to pursue a second career in public service.

The Empty Nest

The bottom line for the marketer is that the Baby Boomer woman is constantly searching for ways to make the most out of each newly experienced life stage. By relating products and services as solutions to her life stage needs, more so than relying solely upon age as the primary criteria, the smart marketer leverages her life-cycle transitions to forge a stronger brand connection at a time when the consumer is more likely to be receptive to new/additional products and services.

The opportunity for life stage marketing is enormous. Never before in history has such a large demographic experienced major life stage transitions en masse as the Baby Boomer generation. Take the empty nest as an example. A critical juncture in a mother's lifecycle, the empty nest phenomenon represents an opportunity for marketers sensitive to the evolving needs, challenges, and heightened emotional landscape of her life.

As a generation, Boomers have embraced a more engaged approach to parenting than was the norm of their parents. These Boomer moms, who have spent the past two decades involved in the predominant nurturing role of raising kids, are strongly affected when the responsibilities of this role shift. Our research draws attention to what many Boomer women experience: that the act of a child leaving home can create a profound sense of loss, self-examination, freedom, and change. (Note: We are not referring to this life stage as the popularly nicknamed "empty nest syndrome," given that not all women experience this new stage in life as a "problem." While there is an admittedly complex emotional component, the "empty nest" is also experienced by many as an opportunity for new life experiences.)

Toyota gets it right with their "Moving Forward" print campaign. One ironically evocative ad shows a college freshman standing with his personal possessions piled in front of his new dorm building. In the background, his parents drive off in their Toyota Highlander. Amidst the rag-tag collection of suitcases, there are skateboards, musical instruments, weights, and a hand-me-down microwave and TV. The headline reads: "5:15 p.m. Dropping the kid off at college. 5:17 p.m. What kid?"

Consider, too, that the emptying nest is not just a one-time occurrence for her—nor is it a one-time marketing opportunity for your company. The emptying of the family's nest is often a layered experience across the coming-of-age of several children, and their progressive separations from college to graduation and beyond. Each child's departure from home is a defining event with a flavor and intensity of its own. Compare the emotions and concerns the Baby Boomer mom is likely to be negotiating when her first child is leaving home, as opposed to the emotional and practical ramifications related to the departure of her last child.

Why should your company care? By deeply understanding the issues she faces, marketers can align their brand to provide her answers at a time of need. Considering the size and spending clout of the Boomer woman demographic, sensitive marketers will stand to benefit from her gratitude.

In the next section, we've summarized our findings and translated key insights from our empty nest research into an example of marketing opportunities targeted to helping her through this complex life stage transition. Participants in the survey primarily represent the core female Baby Boomer consumer.[2]

Feathering the Empty Nest

Newfound Freedom

When asked which were the most significant changes anticipated or experienced once their nest emptied, the overwhelming response (out of 12 possibilities) was "more free time," followed by "loneliness/depression," "more time with significant other," and "focus on self."

Opportunity for Marketers: Emphasize relational aspects, such as girlfriend getaways, renewed romance and self-nurturing experiences. Due in part to tailoring trips and amenities to these empty nester desires, the cruise industry has performed beyond expectations consistently over the past decade.

Mixed Bag of Emotions

While proud of their children's accomplishments and enthusiastic about their children's future, these moms are also equally anxious about their offspring's increasing independence. Simultaneously, they feel conflicted about the changing nature of their relationships with their children and how they will define their own transitioning identity.

Opportunity: Help ease separation anxiety with products and services that keep her in touch with her child's life without seeming invasive. Who says the audience for interactive cell phones, instant messaging, and webcams is 18-34? Boomer moms are wired and eagerly embracing technology that enhances their circle of relationships.

(Take note: Those cool, tiny buttons and electronic micro-text are not popular with bifocaled Boomers. And although they are tech-wise, it is critical that you humanize the experience of using your product to be simple and intuitive.

They have no patience for complex user interfaces or confusing directions.)

Searching for Support

When asked what resources they wished they had to navigate the empty nest stage of life, more than half of the respondents said greater peer support, coach/advisor resources, retreat/workshop opportunities and friendship networks.

Opportunity: Create a supportive community by sponsoring a seminar series or retreat that helps her tackle transition. GlaxoSmithKline teams with consumer product companies, such as Stonyfield Farm, to provide the "Strong Women Summits," helping women step back and reflect on ways to realize their full potential. (You will find more on the Strong Women Summits in Chapter Six.)

Simplifying and Downsizing

Almost 30 percent of the soon-to-be empty nesters surveyed anticipate simplifying or downsizing their lifestyle once the kids leave.[3]

Opportunity: This desire for downsizing has huge implications for the housing and home furnishings industries, as empty nesters adjust their living situation to suit their new lifestyle. They're looking for living options to accommodate this active, second-lease-on-life phase. Some are staying put, converting an empty bedroom into a home office for launching a new business, adding a room for developing new hobbies, or redecorating existing spaces for visiting adult children and grandchildren. Others are downsizing, moving from suburban homes back to small urban apartments within walking distance of cultural amenities, such as theatre and restaurants.

Another example of leveraging the downsizing trend is

Pillsbury's "Cooking for Two" campaign. Aimed at helping Boomers adjust to cooking, buying, and organizing meals for a smaller household, this online resource is a groundbreaking effort to connect directly to this demographic. "We want to ease what can be a challenging transition, providing resources, products and meal planning advice for this new stage of life," says Mark Toth, Pillsbury marketing manager at General Mills.[4]

Pursuing New Experiences

Sixty-six percent of respondents indicated that now that the nest is empty, they want to pursue new experiences. On the top of their list is travel, with other interests including motorcycling, scuba diving, skydiving, mountain climbing, white water rafting, painting, writing, volunteer work, and starting a second career.[5]

Opportunity: Boomer women are more likely than younger demographics to have the means to satisfy their cravings. Entrepreneur and Baby Boomer Bev Sanders has built several businesses on the winning combination of offering women the chance to master a new skill and feed their desire for adventure, while providing the opportunity to engage in both self-discovery and community. After taking up surfing at the age of 44, she launched Las Olas Surf Safaris for Women, followed by Artista Creative Safaris for Women. Who would guess that the majority of her surfers/students are Baby Boomer women?

Another company that has done their homework with this demographic is Principal Financial Group. In an advertisement offering solutions to help female consumers secure their dreams (pension plans, insurance and rollover IRAs, among others), the featured model is a woman 50+, trimly garbed head to toe in a high-tech wet suit, carrying a surfboard overhead.

New experiences, however, can be a double-edged sword. The Baby Boomer woman in her early fifties is likely to experience more life-changing events than at any other time period of her life. While women in this age group are more likely to try new products, services, and experiences, it is also in this same age range that women tend to be the most worried and stressed.

Engaging the Post-Family Guest

The Baby Boomer woman's nest may be empty, but her pocketbook has plenty of disposable income to invest in anything that will help her through this complex and emotional transition period. One company that is addressing this new reality is Walt Disney Parks and Resorts, which sets the pace for life-stage marketing in recognizing the importance of their brand and its longstanding emotional resonance with their guests.

"The most important marketing objective for us is to constantly reinforce this emotional connection by having an ongoing, engaging conversation, utilizing a variety of messaging communication platforms. Nowhere is this more significant than in our marketing outreach to women," says Michael Mendenhall, executive vice president of global marketing for Walt Disney Parks and Resorts.

"We continually strive to recognize and understand segment developments, such as the importance of Boomer women (the most influential generation of women to date) and their never-before-seen influence on financial decisions in today's world."

Research conducted by Walt Disney Parks and Resorts affirms

that women influence 80 percent of all consumer-buying decisions in the United States, and that about three-fourths of these women are mothers. In turn, children influence nearly 50 percent of what mothers spend. For Walt Disney Parks and Resorts, the most important fact is that 92 percent of all vacation purchasing decisions are made by or influenced by women, and that among women with families, 96 percent stated that when they choose where to take their vacation, a key influencer is vacations that "create memories."

"The only way we will be able to continue to exceed expectations, and continue to build and enhance the relationships with our guests, will be to listen to what they are telling us, understand what they are saying, and be nimble enough to tailor our products and services to meet their needs," says Mendenhall. "We are confronting a time when one of the largest and most important target segments for our business is struggling with one of the most challenging life stages they will ever face: Baby Boomer women are regaining their independence as their children move away from home."

Mendenhall continues: "Fundamental societal anxieties such as this have an undeniable impact on our business, but they actually represent phenomenal opportunities for our brand. Whether it is our ability to provide Baby Boomer moms the opportunity for a long overdue adventure, offer ways to keep them connected with their children, or even just present them with exciting options given their newfound freedom, the overarching strategy remains the same."

The philosophy of marketing at Walt Disney Parks and Resorts is that engagement and connection will only come through deep understanding and an "unyielding desire" to personally get to know every guest. Input from their guests has assisted Disney in creating highly successful programs that specifically address what Mendenhall refers to as "the post-family scenario," which will continue to expand as this Baby Boomer generation grows older.

Walt Disney Parks and Resorts marketing has also become more aggressive in establishing and maintaining an ongoing dialogue with guests via detailed guest surveys. These surveys, which have affirmed that the Internet continues to be the most utilized planning tool for moms in researching vacation options, have also captured the information that women today expect to be able to customize the products they buy. The survey feedback led Walt Disney Parks and Resorts to create marketing programs that specifically address the desire for personalization. One such program is "Magic Your Way," a new Walt Disney World Resort ticket medium and vacation package that matches the needs and desires of guests, all based on the premise of the more a guest plays, the less they pay per day.

Disney's research also reveals that 32 percent of travelers have taken a multigenerational trip and that 12 percent have attended an off-site family reunion. Having proactively identified this societal trend, Disney responded by developing "Magical Gatherings," a multifaceted program designed to help large families and groups organize their visits and get the most from their Walt Disney World Resort vacations.

"It's an ideal program for empty-nest Baby Boomer moms wishing to reconnect with their extended families (kids, grandchildren, and valued friends)," says Mendenhall, whose marketing successes include the opening of Hong Kong Disneyland and the global celebration of Disneyland's 50th anniversary.

"Through the years, the Disney vacation experience has become a rite of passage—a special experience passed down from generation to generation. By consistently delivering and exceeding the expectations of our guests for a safe, memorable, and quality experience, and by remaining relevant to and in touch with the needs of our guests, we will be able to connect successfully with our female audience in emotional, thought-provoking ways, proving the old adage that 'Mom is always right!' "

Painting Her Life Stage Portraits

The empty nest is just one of the life stages that marketers of products and services should keep in mind in relation to the Baby Boomer woman. Referring to the life-stage chart presented earlier in Figure 3-1, you now know that she is apt to be balancing career and family, going back to school, thinking about retirement, starting her own business, taking stock of her life, being the caretaker for an extended multigenerational family, and/or seeking self-improvement of body, mind, and spirit—many of these in full-swing simultaneously. And that's just for starters.

We are about to paint a series of life stage portraits of the core female Baby Boomer consumer. Painted with broad strokes on the basis of demographic, industry, and category-specific statistics, the following portraits illustrate how life stage and generational influences tend to play out in five important categories.

1. Body and Soul
2. Work and Money
3. Leisure and Travel
4. Home and Family
5. Technology

In addition to the broad-stroke criteria used to develop the following templates, marketers will want to keep in mind that the consumer portrait they paint for their own purposes may differ slightly or tremendously. This will depend on cultural and economic factors deemed by them to be of particular importance in regards to their specific products or services. What is critical for the marketer to keep in mind at this juncture is how important—and helpful—it is to breathe life into the statistics that can be gleaned about her, synthesizing the complex influences, dynamics and intelligence into an accessible portrait of her that will be product or category specific.

We begin with the category of Body and Soul, recalling that Trailing-Edge Boomers, the younger demographic, are in their 40s and early 50s, while Leading-Edge Boomers, the older demographic, are in their mid-50s and just entering their early 60s.

1. Body and Soul

Portrait of the Trailing-Edge Boomer

Redefining Fitness

Sprinting to the next staff meeting then out to a fundraiser or home to prepare dinner for the family isn't the only way this busy woman gets her heart rate up. Having gratefully emerged from the era of Army-style gym classes and five-times-a-week studio aerobics, she's now embracing more soulful fitness activities including Pilates, yoga, and active walking. In the spirit of her modus operandi, multitasking, these pursuits are not only easier on her body, but they are emotionally soothing and empowering at the same time. Stretch and meditate simultaneously? Work her heart while learning self-defense techniques? She's in. Most importantly, she looks for situations where she can leverage a reduced schedule of classes with at-home or lunch-hour practice, on her own terms and at her own pace. Maybe it's the "Madonna" factor, too, but between 2000 and 2004, yoga participation increased 122 percent,[6] with the largest group of female practitioners being 45- to 54-years old.[7]

If she has children, chances are they're no longer infants. She's free to leave the house, getting out on her own or with friends to enjoy some fresh air. Outdoor sports challenge her muscles and give her an emotional shot of physical accomplishment. Adventure sports such as hiking and mountain biking are drawing her to the trails and boosting her sense of strength and achievement. Coming up fast as well, according to contributing author Fran Philip, chief merchandising officer of L.L. Bean, is snow-shoeing.

Marketing to Her

This energetic group has redefined the meaning of fitness. Talk to her about healthy activity that can take place outside of the gym and in her living room, on a mountainside trail or spa-like setting, combining spirituality and physical conditioning. Give her comfort, performance, and style. Recognize her as a serious athlete who needs innovative fitness gear, apparel, and facilities to enhance her physical accomplishments. Tailor your products to fit her body and her lifestyle, and she'll respond with loyalty and enthusiasm.

Brands including Title 9 Sports, Nuala yoga wear, and Terry Bicycles have thrived with her by creating high performance, style-savvy merchandise designed *by* women *for* women. And Curves—the women-only fitness center—has become the world's largest fitness center franchise almost exclusively through word-of-mouth referrals. Curves offers an on-demand, 30-minute workout in a bar-ebones, yet encouraging environment. The busy woman can grab a half-hour on her way to work, during her lunch hour, or whenever the moment can be seized. Capitalizing on this formula for success, Curves has expanded its franchises by 560 percent since 1999 and started an explosive movement of women-centric fitness centers.[8]

The bottom line? Make it easy for her to fit exercise into her life—and give it a multitasking purpose—and you'll capture the affection of this resourceful, fitness-oriented woman.

The Flip Side

Trailing-Edge Boomers are exercising far more than past generations at age 40+. But it's still an uphill struggle for them to find the time and motivation. Faced with a massive to-do list, exercise quickly slips out of the picture, as today nearly 40 percent of women say they always feel rushed versus 28 percent in 1975.[9]

Portrait of the Leading-Edge Boomer

Fitness as the Foundation of the Well-Lived Life

As she blows out more candles on her (low-fat, low-carb) birthday cake, this woman is embracing the physical aspects of middle age and beyond with a whole new mindset. With her kids grown and more time to invest on herself, she's focused on getting healthier, feeling stronger, and renewing her body and spirit with each passing year. In fact, 7 in 10 Boomer women feel a lot younger than their actual age, and 62 percent say they work at trying to maintain a youthful appearance.[10]

She's still busy, however, and in some ways—sandwiched as she is between the conflicting demands of grown children and aging parents—she is more in need of serenity than ever. Her medicine cabinet and make-up table are stocked with beauty and skin products that simplify, rather than complicate, her everyday routine.

Her kitchen cabinet tells a similar story. Because of her responsiveness to the benefits of health foods, she can find items that were once relegated to the specialty stores but are now on her favorite supermarket's shelves. This is a one-stop shopping boon for the busy woman grabbing something fast and now healthy on the way home from work. She'll even pay a higher price for products that are healthful, but she's not willing to sacrifice taste in the process.

She's also got the cash and will make the time to visit the spa, purchase alternative and allopathic health products, and enjoy the latest beauty treatments.

Marketing to Her

Embrace her passion for youthfulness and vitality, but market to her wisdom and her well-honed sense of self. No Hollywood diets or miracle creams will fly here. Develop ongoing relationships that authentically address her health and beauty maintenance concerns.

Kiehl's has created an almost cultish following for its prestigious hair and skincare products with relationship marketing and product sampling, bare bones packaging, and no advertising whatsoever. *O*, the Oprah magazine, and Oprah.com are two other wildly successful brands for this Boomer woman. With the "live your best life" slogan, Oprah uses her multimedia channels to provide feel-good emotions, information, and insights about body and soul in a hip, interactive format.

The marketing message is clear. Focus on how your product or service helps her quest for inner wisdom, health, and beauty, and you may develop a cult-like following of your own.

The Flip Side

"Embrace yourself, not your age" may be this woman's mantra, but she's still struggling with the changes she sees in the mirror, and with the physical side of aging. While 61 percent of women believe that older women can be more attractive than younger ones, 48 percent think they looked their best in their 20s.[11] Simply look at the span from the late 1990s to the turn of the century, when the number of Americans undergoing plastic surgery had increased by a whopping 1,125 percent.[12] (Statistics don't lie—but recall Cheryl Tiegs' comment to Katie Couric on *The Today Show*: "I think the days of plastic surgery, pulling everything back, getting rid of every single line and wrinkle, are over." For more on the nature of this conversation that is taking place among Baby Boomer, see Chapter Four.)

2. Work and Money

Portrait of the Trailing-Edge Boomer

Money Maven

When it comes to managing the household finances, this woman is in control. She is also the one who brings home a good chunk of the family income.[13] She's more focused on her career than her mother or her grandmothers ever were, and she's very likely to be taking night classes to finish off her undergrad or to complete a graduate degree. Her work often requires travel, and she uses business trips as a chance to rest and recharge her batteries—away from the chaos and responsibilities of home.

This woman is also far more financially savvy then her mother ever was. She learns about the stock market and upgrades her money know-how with information from books, friends, the Web, and other reliable sources such as women's investment clubs.

Marketing to Her

Concerned about both her short- and long-term well-being, she wants to learn about investment opportunities. She also knows that the statistics can be daunting. Women earn 76 cents for each dollar men earn[14] and live an average of seven years longer, with typically higher healthcare expenses.[15]

What does this mean for the marketer? Opportunities abound if you keep her consumption patterns in mind. She wants to conduct thorough research before committing to an investment, and spends 40 percent more time than men researching a fund before investing her hard-earned dollars.[16] Ease her time-crunch by losing the jargon and abandoning financial hype. Give her small portions of information in digestible pieces and familiar language. Suze Orman's television program, and the online site Motley Fool, have become popular with this demographic by tackling real-life, familiar financial issues with a straightforward, question-and-answer format. (Again, satisfying the multitasking woman's urge for one-stop shopping, Orman throws spiritual advice in for good measure.)

Keep in mind that the Trailing-Edge Boomer is doing much more than paying the bills or taking out a low-risk mutual fund. Women represent nearly half of all investors with $100,000 or more in assets worthy of investment, and more than half are financially independent.[17]

The Flip Side

As attuned as they are to financial information, this group of women knows that they need more. According to a survey by the American Institute of Certified Public Accountants, seven in ten women say they need help managing their finances. Another 76 percent of women say they have credit card debt, and 35 percent use their cards frequently and carry balances.

Portrait of the Leading-Edge Boomer

Switching Gears

This woman is in her peak earning years, thanks to solid work experience and her focus on education. She's got an undergraduate and maybe even a master's degree, and has consistently leveraged her "down time" to attend conferences and seminars that enhance her career—not to mention her personal development. She's made real progress within the corporate structure, but now she's at a crossroads. What's ahead?

This highly driven woman refined her skills in the corporate womb, but now she's ready for an entrepreneurial opportunity and the challenge of starting her own business. Running the show would give her the flexibility to dedicate more time to her extended family, her community, and herself. And time is a key consideration. Starting her business will still require a major time investment, but it's a way to explore her personal passions and test her limits—opportunities that her previous career may no longer offer.

Marketing to Her

Smart companies will tailor their business products and services to accommodate this busy, entrepreneurial woman. Remember that while she may be switching gears, she's hardly a novice.

KeyBank has capitalized on the growth of women-owned business by launching "Key4Women," a nationwide program offering access to customized resources, online tools, and account and service suggestions. With a promise to "help your business grow," Key has reinforced its commitment to female entrepreneurs by cosponsoring a study of $1 million+ female business success stories, conducted by the Center for Women's Business Research. (For more about KeyBank's innovative programming, see Chapter Four.)

Understand the major differences between women and men in entrepreneurial roles and you can reach your share of this lucrative market. The number of women-owned businesses is growing at twice the rate of all U.S. firms.[18] In addition, women are more likely than men to rely on the Internet for its ability to open up new business opportunities and to enhance time flexibility.[19] For example, real estate guru Barbara Corcoran's phone seminars provide adaptable delivery options and great online service by allowing time-starved women to call in at their convenience.

The Flip Side

Not every woman is ready to strike out as an entrepreneur or to abandon her role in the corporate fold. Women not only comprise 46.6 percent of the U.S. labor force,[20] but women 50+ account for more than 22 percent of the female workforce.[21] In addition, 68 percent of women age 50 to 59 are currently in the labor force,[22] and 22 percent of these working women over 50 plan never to retire.[23]

3. Leisure and Travel

Portrait of the Trailing-Edge Boomer

Household CTC

With two weeks of vacation on the calendar, she's busy planning the next family trip. As the household CFO, CEO, and CTC (Corporate

Travel Coordinator), this multitasking woman researches and coordinates a dizzying range of excursions. Increasingly, she's doing that research online—after reloading the dishwasher, starting another load of laundry, and helping the kids with their homework. The Internet is her key resource, and she's not alone. Of women online, 65 percent use the Web to purchase or arrange travel reservations[24] and 71 percent utilize it to conduct their travel research.[25]

Travel is her way of reconnecting with herself, her loved ones, and the world at large. It's time away from the everyday routine, and a chance to "check in" and take stock of her life. Travel is truly critical to her state of mind, whether the family drives to Grandma's house in Vermont, or they all fly together to Disneyland.

Marketing to Her

If you want influence, you've got to reach the family CTC. Women make the majority of travel decisions, regardless of who pays for the trip, where they go, or who's accompanying them. In total, Boomer women generate more travel than any other age group in the United States.

How can you attract and retain this woman's travel dollars? Understand the amenities she's looking for in a family trip or business travel and work with her most important decision point, whether it's price, value, location, or services. Market to her key concern and communicate with her in the process. Recognize how she arranges her travel, and make her planning experience a whole lot easier and more enjoyable.

The Flip Side

She's still booking her travel online, but her next trip may involve room service, the latest pay-per-view movie, and a full schedule of meetings. As of 2005, women comprised 50 percent of the business travel market.[26] Also remember, she may be traveling on business, but she constantly has her radar up for other forms of travel. She's considering whether or not your services could cater to her family travel (60 percent of all trips with children are taken by women age 35 to 54)[27] or if your product is the perfect spot for her next girlfriend getaway.

Portrait of the Leading-Edge Boomer

Indiana Jane

She still regales her family with stories of backpacking through Europe on pocket change, or if she didn't actually get there, she's still dreaming of buying a Eurail pass, albeit probably in first class, and hitting the road. Now that the kids are becoming self-sufficient, this woman has the time and money to satisfy her wanderlust. As a Baby Boomer, she spends more on her travel than any other age group, averaging $491 per trip, excluding transportation to her destination.[28] She's also often more likely to travel solo or with her girlfriends than with a spouse.

For this woman, travel is all about adventure and learning. She wants both a physical and a spiritual journey. What fits the bill? A week-long cooking class in Venice, botanical and wildlife painting in exotic locales, an all-female cycling tour through New England, or a yoga retreat in Costa Rica? As the number of women-only tour operators has grown by 230 percent in the last six years,[29] she's finding more companies that understand her twin desires for sightseeing and self-understanding.

Marketing to Her

Travel and outdoor magazines may feature glossy photos of fit twixters climbing peaks and fording streams, but the average adventure traveler is a 54-year-old woman.[30]

Indiana Jane is ready to spend money on travel if she'll get a truly authentic experience in return. Give her comprehensive, detailed travel information, virtual tours, related resources, educational tie-ins, and testimonials that take her there ahead of time and give her a vivid sense of what she's going to see and do. Satisfy both her adventurous and her practical sides. Highlight learning and the environmental, rejuvenating, or cultural benefits of the locale. Give her value for her dollar, and provide a unique, memorable, and restful experience that sends her home with more than just tan lines and a suitcase full of souvenirs.

The Flip Side

This woman is seeking adventure, but she's also up for some serious R&R, as women comprise 71 percent of spa goers.[31] But don't assume she's heading to a romantic dinner after that seaweed scrub and Shiatsu massage. Thirty-one percent of trips taken by Baby Boomer households include at least one child or grandchild.[32] They'll want to know that the facility they're booking has both a waterslide and a spa.

4. Home and Family

Portrait of the Trailing-Edge Boomer

Homeowner Handywoman

Her weekend is all lined up. First, she's off to Home Depot for a Saturday morning Women's Workshop, then it's back home to install those nickel-plated bathroom faucets. After applying a fresh coat of paint, she'll achieve that Pottery Barn perfect bath effect she's envisioned. From magazines to TV to the Internet, she's constantly gathering new ideas and refining her project list.

This do-it-yourself woman is hitting the toolbox to save money, but more importantly, it's a great way to ensure things get done the way *she* wants them done. It feels good to hone her skills and to get comfortable with a power saw. That's why she's got the next three Women's Workshops penciled on her calendar—even though she probably won't have time to attend all of them.

Marketing to Her

Think these women are merely helping their husbands or hiring the contractor? Think again. Women are driving the entire process, eager, active participants in home remodeling. In fact, they initiate 80 percent of all home improvement purchase decisions, especially big-ticket items such as kitchen cabinets, flooring, and bathroom fixtures.[33] Moreover, home ownership among single women has increased, and women in married couples frequently control the household spending.

The Flip Side

Women have always had a grip on the hammer. The National Association of Women in Construction was founded in Fort Worth, Texas in 1953. It has 5,500 members and more than 179 chapters in forty-eight U.S. states and in three Canadian provinces. The news here is not so much that women are taking care of business around the house, but that marketers have recognized this and have become less fearful of losing their male customers by catering more to women in the marketplace.

Portrait of the Leading-Edge Boomer

Ultimate Caretaker

She's just as interested in getting the house just right—but since she moved out of the big family home to the cozy condo, there's less house to fix.

Family members may no longer be living at home, but she's

added her own children's significant others, their children, and an even larger network of relationships into the fabric of her life. From hunting down the perfect birthday card to providing around-the-clock care during flu season, this woman is selfless and nurturing. She's a dedicated mother (even though her children are grown), sister, daughter, cousin, aunt, friend, and neighbor. She sees herself as the primary caretaker, even for the family pet.

She moves through the world with her friends and family in mind—from picking up an extra copy of that great cooking magazine for her sister, to finding a later Pilates class so she can attend her grandson's soccer game. For 96 percent of women, having a healthy family rates among their top priority,[34] and two-thirds of women put time with family and friends ahead of their personal health care.[35]

But just when she's figured out how to juggle all her social roles and responsibilities, caring for an aging parent can further complicate her life. Faced head-on with the failing health of elder relations (or family members), she realizes that she needs to plan for her future and avoid becoming a burden to her own children.

Marketing to Her

Help strengthen her connections with loved ones and streamline her multiple social roles. If she's caring for aging parents or extended family with special needs, she'll hunt relentlessly for anything that can boost their quality of life or that will make her a more effective caregiver. By the way, forget about marketing incontinence products, medical alert systems, and the like to her ailing parents, so frequently appealed to directly by advertisers as the logical consumer of these products. Instead, target the Baby Boomer woman with the information she needs to provide her parents with products and services that will make all of their lives easier. In this case, she's the real consumer. (And while she won't be likely to admit it, she's watching everything you do as she makes mental notes about who will be the marketplace players in her own unfolding future.)

The Flip Side
Boomers had fewer children than their parents, leaving a shortage of adult children to act as caregivers when the time arrives. Marketers who have solutions to this issue, such as developers of cooperative housing developments designed specifically for single Boomer women in their fifties and up, will find a receptive audience for their products.

5. Technology

Portrait of the Trailing-Edge Boomer

Cyber Savvy Sophisticate
When she's not researching her next handheld photo printer or techno-gadget, this woman harnesses the Web to smooth the wrinkles in her busy life. She's going online to shop, track down information, research, and send e-mails to her friends and family. She's part of the most consumer-educated demographic surfing the Internet, and it's quickly becoming her top retail destination—whether or not she actually buys merchandise from an e-commerce site. In fact, 78 percent of women say they use the Internet to research a product before hitting the cash register.[36] For this multitasking maven, the Web is not a toy. It's a tool, available 24/7 to take advantage of those unpredictable free moments and rare pockets of downtime.

Marketing to Her
Women have flocked to the Internet in huge numbers, making them, at 51.6 percent, the majority of users.[37] Add to this the fact that the

35- to 45-year-old group has the largest online representation,[38] and your opportunity becomes clear. Compared to men, women have showed more growth in online activities.[39] Think about how you can serve their cyber needs with style and simplicity, and you'll gain a strong following with this highly-wired demographic.

The Flip Side

Baby Boomer women may be researching new products on the Web, but they tend to be newer to the Internet and spend less time online. When they do surf, it's more likely to be a search for medical, fitness, weight loss, and spiritual information from the comfort of her home. And while women may be dominating the Internet, keep in mind that men account for 42 percent of total visitors to women's sites.[40] Men are also less likely than women to say a bad website would lead them to shop elsewhere.

Portrait of the Leading-Edge Boomer

Digital Diva

With the kids edging their way out of the family nest—and with her discretionary income on the rise—this woman is the "hidden powerhouse" in e-commerce. She's using the Internet at home and at work—where she's making travel arrangements, doing research, and scanning the latest headlines from her office.

While she may be surfing, she's certainly not playing. Novelty is not a factor here. Instead, a full 83 percent of women say they use the Internet to save time, and another 55 percent go online to save money.[41] She's using the Internet even more heavily than the wired moms in her neighborhood, and she gives her credit card a workout by spending more at her favorite online stores.

Marketing to Her

Talk about growth potential. Boomer women were raised on catalog shopping, and now there's a whole new world of digital choices at their fingertips. In 2003, online retail sales totaled $52.6 billion, with women making up 52 percent of online shoppers.[42] This group is ready to spend, but you've got to keep it simple. Don't waste her time with pop-ups, complicated navigation, or fussy design.

The Flip Side

This woman may be the hidden powerhouse of e-commerce, but she's already embraced technology in her daily life. The hottest tech items for women over 40 are cell phones, digital cameras, DVD players, and computers. Forty-seven percent of women in this age group said they recently bought or will soon buy a wireless phone; 45 percent said they just purchased a digital camera or will soon buy one; and 42 percent named a DVD player as a recent or near-future purchase.[43]

On High Technology Marketing to Women

Gina Clark,

Vice President of Internet Communications, Product Marketing

LOGITECH

Internet communications products are an important part of what Logitech does. Because relationships are at the core of communications, and relationships are something that are particularly important to Baby Boomer women, we at Logitech have a great deal of interest in learning how to develop and market our Internet communications products to Baby Boomer women.

Historically, the high technology industry has catered to people—generally males—who like to tinker with technology. In the past decade, this has changed as technology has matured and, most recently, as the mass-market has formed for Internet communications products. Mass-market growth has been fueled by the adoption of broadband and the availability of free, video communications services. Baby Boomer women have embraced the Internet for communications, information gathering, and shopping.

As we conducted market research we discovered that Baby Boomer women made up a healthy part of our user base—not surprising since our products focus on video and audio communications. As a result it made sense to further understand what Baby Boomer women want regarding Internet communications products, not only because they are the family communicators, but also because of their buying power and influence over all household spending.

Our research made it clear to us that Baby Boomer women do have specific needs but that these needs would in fact make our products better for men as well as women. We learned that women simply wanted products that work and they were looking for complete solutions—they weren't looking for just the top one or two features. Quality and functionality were both important. We thought there might be special features we could create to target women but our research showed that this wasn't necessary. In fact, some features might be perceived as gimmicks, which would contradict the quality and simplicity that women were looking for.

We also had concerns about whether our traditional electronics channels would reach women. The reality is that women often ask family members to help them with their technology purchases. In addition, consumer electronics retailers are investing in specialized personal shoppers who can help women navigate the technology aisles. Therefore, developing new channels wouldn't be necessary.

So it may sound like we really didn't have to change all that much to appeal to women and to increase our market share with Baby Boomer women, but the truth is more complex than that. To reach Baby Boomer women, we would need to expand our marketing mix to encompass woman-oriented programming, online sites, and publications. These were not traditionally in our standard marketing mix. We would need to concentrate our messaging more on benefits versus product features—a change that again would help us communicate more effectively across the board. Personal recommendations from friends and family members are important to women, therefore, public relations would be a primary vehicle for marketing to women.

There are challenges within a high-technology company in marketing to women. First, there has to be internal education on what it means to develop and market products to Baby Boomer women. The first reaction might be, "Do we have to put products in the cosmetics aisle or in shoe stores?" Fear of the unknown is real. There can also be some inertia, because clearly women bought products in the past, so why do anything special now? The simple answer is that Baby Boomer women make up a growing part of an affluent segment that can result in market growth, and focus will create better results.

To sum up, marketing to Baby Boomer women presents a few challenges. It will always be easier to keep doing things the way you've done them in the past, but the changes required to develop and market products to Boomer women will benefit the company overall. You have to stay true to your vision to develop and market products to Baby Boomer women by becoming the evangelist within your company.

There will be resistance. Most importantly, understand the Boomer woman market and don't assume that you know what women want, even if you are a woman.

Gina Clark is responsible for the product marketing strategy for Logitech's line of PC headsets, webcams, and related live video and audio software. She is also responsible for delivering innovative products that meet customer needs and by promoting the integration of Logitech's products with key Internet communication applications and services. Ms. Clark works with key strategic partners such as Skype and Microsoft globally to ensure that customers receive the best solutions. Prior to joining Logitech, Gina was the vice president of business development and marketing for Steve Wozniak's startup, Wheels of Zeus, and has also worked with Apple Computer and Palm, Inc.

Operationalizing the Portraits

The five portraits discussed above are a point-of-entry for marketers who are serious about getting to know their consumers. Having even a broadstroke life stage portrait in hand is certainly a giant leap forward for those who previously based their strategies on age alone.

Appleseed's, a retailer of apparel targeted to women 50+, is one company that is reaping the benefits of building segmented consumer personas based on multiple data stream that take into consideration both generational and life stage influences.

On the Power of Creating Brand Personas

Claire Spofford,

Senior Vice President of Marketing and Retail

APPLESEED'S

Appleseed's has been providing quality, classic apparel to woman across the United States for sixty years. Our market historically has been women 50+. But things began to change when the women of the Baby Boomer generation starting turning 50. Appleseed's knew that in order to continue growing, we needed to understand the generational differences between our traditional customer and this new demographic.

Baby Boomers grew up under a different set of expectations and influencers than did the preceding generation. Specifically with regard to apparel, twenty years ago women in their 50s and 60s didn't wear jeans. Boomer women, on the other hand, have grown up in jeans and are very comfortable in them. Nevertheless, as these women are maturing, their bodies are changing. Yet, they are no longer willing to give up comfort for style—or vice versa.

In order to really understand who this Baby Boomer customer is, we've made a substantial investment for a company of our size in consumer research. Internal and transactional data about customers is extremely beneficial, but in terms of thinking about the future, companies need to balance this valuable data with a realistic look at the marketplace. We embarked on a benchmark study of 800 qualified women between the ages of 50 and 75 who are or could be our shoppers. We tried to limit the phone interviews to 25 minutes or less. But these women were so excited about being asked their opinions that the average interview was 43 minutes!

From our research, we discovered that there is a clear segmentation within this group of women based on how they describe their sense of personal style. By focusing on the strongest segment, we gave shape to the core Appleseed's customer persona, whom we refer to as "Kate." Kate is classic in her style, yet doesn't want to look like she's wearing a uniform. She wants personal touches and special details so that she can put her own looks together. She's interested in comfort and ease-of-care and dresses more casually than she used to. Kate is also willing to invest in quality and open to exploring new brands. She is a suburban mother with grown children and possibly grandchildren.

Our research also revealed another distinct complimentary subsegment, whom we call "Beverly." Beverly is a bit older, more conservative, and content with her look and style. As a result, she is comfortable with the brands she has purchased for a long time, and so not as apt to experiment. Beverly complements the Appleseed's brand, but is different enough to warrant a separate, sister brand. We found the perfect match in The Tog Shop, purchasing the brand in 2005. As a result, we are able to build bridges to two different, yet powerfully influential segments within our target market.

We can now look within these defined segments, analyze our transactional data, and see which products are working disproportionately well for Kate and which for Beverly. We also use the personas to shape and drive the look and feel of our catalogs and websites. From model selection and product assortment, to page layout, type font and messaging, we consider what we know appeals to each persona.

It is important to keep in mind that when you create personas, you are, by necessity, making generalizations. It is impossible to say that every Boomer woman is exactly the same—we've learned that they are absolutely not. Beverly and Kate are helpful tools, but the women in our research study spelled it out loud and clear to us: Understand who I am, let me know you care about my needs and that my opinions matter to you.

Claire Spofford joined Appleseed's in 2003 as senior vice president of marketing and retail. Her responsibilities include marketing, retail stores, catalog creative, and production. From 1993 to 2003 Claire served in various capacities at The Timberland Company, including vice president of global marketing. From 1991 to 1993 she worked in marketing at Boston Whaler. Claire graduated from University of Vermont and holds a master's degree in business administration from Babson College. She lives on Boston's North Shore with her husband and two children. Claire serves on the board of directors at Project Adventure, a nonprofit organization focused on improving the lives of youth through adventure-based learning.

We are now ready to take an even deeper dive beyond generational cohorts and life stage drivers. In the next chapter, we take you to the cutting edge of psychological, spiritual and developmental research, explaining motivational archetypes for Baby Boomer women that will help you get to know her from the inside out.

CHAPTER FOUR

She's Motivated

The 3-D View of Her

In Chapter Three, we shared a series of broad-stroke portraits of the Baby Boomer woman with you, considering her life stage challenges and generational influences. But this is not the whole story, for within each life stage, psychological, social, and even spiritual factors will have an impact, both consciously and subconsciously, on the individual woman's receptivity to products and services. What is needed is a 3-D view of her that takes an even deeper dive into the very heart of marketing: what is motivating her purchasing decisions on the archetypal level.

On Appealing to Her Psyche

Michael Bohn,

Director of Brand Marketing (Bosch, Siemens, Thermador, Gaggenau)

BSH HOME APPLIANCES CORPORATION

Demographic segmentation criteria like age need to be augmented by deeper insight into consumer lifestyles. A progressive city dweller, age 50, likely has more in common with the 30-year-old social activist next door than with her 48-year-old fellow Boomer in rural Kentucky, deeply rooted in a conservative belief system. Consequently, at BSH North America we segment our target market psychographically. Then, we utilize our portfolio of four upscale brands—Bosch, Siemens, Gaggenau, and Thermador—to achieve the closest possible fit with each audience, and each type of female Boomer.

As an example, the Thermador brand is designed to appeal to Leading-Edge Boomers with empty nest concerns like connecting, questing, finding new passions, new ways of expressing her individuality, and redefining the role she plays in life. The Bosch brand, on the other hand, is geared more towards Trailing-Edge Boomer women who find themselves sandwiched between eldercare, childcare and their own career, constantly multitasking. What she needs is not a hobby or a means of socializing, but a highly efficient problem-solver in her kitchen. Consequently, Bosch products (and marketing) emphasize convenience, ease of use, and brilliant results with the least amount of effort and the least infraction on the already busy household (thus, for example, Bosch's emphasis on extremely low noise emission).

Another example of differences between Baby Boomers is their social and political belief system. The cultural rift in this generation, originally opened by the Vietnam War, is still manifesting itself in differing views and attitudes today. In this respect, one brand—such as Thermador with its classic American iconography and its emphasis on heritage—will appeal to a different group from the Bosch brand with a subtle VW-like countercultural "force of good" identity and its open embrace of environmental causes, or from the Siemens brand with its irreverent "forward thinking" campaign. Finally, Boomers simply differ in the style of home or kitchen they prefer. Consequently, our product design and marketing caters to these very divergent style expectations—from the ultra-modern, Euro-designed Gaggenau to the classic American style of Thermador.

One campaign that has resonated particularly well with Baby Boomer women recently is the Thermador brand campaign. Both the underlying positioning strategy and the creative strategy is deeply rooted in the brand's heritage, essentially reinterpreting successful campaigns of decades past in a fresh, new way suited to a new consumer mindset, but consistent with the Thermador brand identity.

The Thermador campaign does not show kitchens. It depicts glamorous, empowered, iconic women of ageless sophistication—together with a Thermador: bold, heroic, and unique. Naturally, this creates visual differentiation, but more than that, it creates a distinct message. It connects in a different way by speaking to needs and desires that are more relevant than just owning a good-looking kitchen. The campaign gets at the deeper emotional needs of its audience. All her life, the typical female has put somebody else first. Now it's about her. Baby Boomer women feel young and want nothing to do with traditional views of "senior life." Indulge them. Give them a sense of empowerment and sex appeal. For all her self-confidence, she is at a time in her life in which she struggles with a perceived loss of control—physically (health) and psychologically (emptying nest, reduced media attention to her generation). A campaign that gives her a feeling of control connects emotionally.

This idea of "empowerment" recently even spawned a revolutionary new refrigeration product concept, the Thermador Freedom Collection, giving the consumer total freedom in making the kitchen of her dreams a reality. But the campaign is about more than kitchen design and performance benefits. It helps shatter traditional assumptions of senior life. In fact, part of its success is due to the fact that it does not directly address the issue of age at all. It shows empowered, sophisticated women of ageless beauty.

Another, more palpable success factor of the campaign is its calculated use of iconic imagery, reminiscent of an era of unprecedented confidence and affluence in American history. Boomers revered icons of beauty and success, and they believed in big dreams. This is the generation that reached for the stars (and attained them), and Thermador's imagery evokes this era—a simpler and safer time in our nation's history, at least in retrospect. Classic in style, contemporary in tone. Just like its audience. That's the formula employed in these ads.

It has been suggested that the Thermador campaign is really a state-of-the-art reinterpretation of 1950's advertising. And maybe that is at the heart of its success. It evokes positive feelings deeply ingrained in Baby Boomers' psyche, but at the same time addresses the emotional issues they have today.

Michael Bohn is responsible for all marketing activities of the Bosch, Siemens, Gaggenau, and Thermador brands in North America. Prior to his current position, he served as head of International Brand Marketing for Siemens at BSH global headquarters in Munich, Germany. In addition to bachelor's and master's degrees in business from the University of Bayreuth in Germany, he earned an MBA degree from the University of Georgia.

The Cutting Edge of Marketing

Motivational marketing represents the cutting edge for companies, with psychosocial research playing an increasingly important role in defining the consumer marketplace. Retail analysts are among those who predict that within the coming years, demographics will no longer be the primary determinant in defining the consumer marketplace. Instead, as a result of diversification and segmentation, motivation and shopping behavior will play increasingly more influential roles.[1]

On Embracing Both Her Demographic and Psychographic Drivers

Grant J. Schneider,

Chief Marketing Officer, Corporate Sales and Marketing

TIME INC.

The women of the Baby Boomer generation have freedoms that previous generations didn't have. They're living lives of their choosing, not lives that were handed to them. This is a fundamental difference from their mothers and grandmothers. Consequently, Boomer women are joining life in very different ways. In general, they are driven by a sense of worth, esteem, and accomplishment that was heretofore unavailable.

You need to connect with her by helping her solve daily life challenges in a very real way in relevance and context, which means it's imperative to understand what's driving her. These women, especially the younger Trailing-Edge Boomers, live a life of duality in a very time-pressed context. They are choosing to do it all: have a career, raise a family, get divorced, remarry, be a single mom. Because she just gets busier and busier, it eliminates the "me" portion of a woman's quadrant of career, family, community, and friends, to the point she feels there's very little "me" left in her life.

In building a case for leading a life less complex, I helped birth *Real Simple* magazine five years ago. The tremendous success of this magazine is due in part to its relevance in speaking to the psychographic issues these women face. When she buys *Real Simple*, she's saying, "I'm part of this club of needing an easier life." Interestingly, we've found this trend has great appeal across multiple generations. *Real Simple* is one of the few magazines in the country that has equal readership numbers among women 25 to 35, 35 to 45, and 45 to 55 years old. Furthermore, of all our magazines, *Real Simple* has the highest rate of gifting: daughters give it to grandmothers, mothers give it to daughters, girlfriends gift it to one another. By moving beyond just demographic concerns, we've tapped into a growing universal trend in women's lives.

Grant Schneider, as chief marketing officer of Time Inc., is charged with delivering creative solutions that leverage the world's most trusted media brands and resources. With an extensive background in marketing and strategic planning, Schneider holds an industry-wide reputation as a power brand-builder. His recently released book, *She Means Business*, harnesses the unparalleled proprietary market research of Time Inc.'s women's magazines to paint a complete and up-to-date portrait of the American female consumer. Prior to this appointment in December 2005, Schneider was vice president, marketing and brand strategy for *Real Simple*.

Motivational Factors

Later in this chapter, we present a diagnostic tool for marketers that helps identify one of three dominant motivational archetypes for the Boomer woman who is most likely to be a candidate for your products or services. But first, we will share the findings of our proprietary study of motivational factors that have an impact on her decision-making processes, behaviors, and attitudes.

As we said in Chapter One, the notion that women 40+ are in a dynamic period of psychosocial growth is revolutionary. Until recently in both scholarly and marketing circles, this period in a woman's life was largely considered to be a developmental wasteland. By the time she approached menopause—and certainly thereafter—she had traditionally been thought to have become long established in her ways. Stable, serene, or, at the very least, marginalized, she was stereotyped as an undesirable target market and, in the eyes of most marketers, invisible.

On Aspiring at Midlife

Peggy Northrop,
Editor-in-Chief

Brenda Saget Darling,
Publisher

***MORE* MAGAZINE**

Women over 40 have plenty of aspirations—but the acceptance of that notion has lagged. Our readers want to be seen as women who still care about how they look, who still care about style, who still care about beauty, but who don't want to look 20 anymore. Our readers get very annoyed when they see products like wrinkle cream shown on a 20-year-old's face. "*I'm sorry. You're 20. You don't need wrinkle cream. Don't try to sell me that.*" But if they see a woman who looks like them, but a little bit better, they have a sense of what it means to aspire to be the best that we can be for our age.

More targets women 40 to 60 years old. Over the past six years, we've grown from 300,000 to 1.1 million, more than tripling our circulation. Our sweet spot falls between the ages of 45 to 54, going to the very heart of the Baby Boomer demographic. While there are life stage and situational differences between the woman on the Trailing- and Leading-Edges of our readership, there is an interesting dynamic that has driven the growth of our circulation among the younger group. We have found that these readers, who are just turning 40, are often doing so with a fair amount of trepidation. They look to our magazine as a way to allay their fears, countering all the messages they get everywhere else, that turning 40 is the beginning of the end. As problem-solvers, juggling the multiple demands of work and family, our younger demographic is inspired by the photos and stories of women who are ten or fifteen years older than they are.

When we put attractive, successful women on our covers who look like they are between their late 40s and mid 50s, we sell lots more copies than when we go for the "40, could pass for 32" look. In fact, one of our highest selling issues of the past year had a great looking 53-year-old, gray-haired woman on the cover. You can see the crinkles around her eyes. We have to restrain our photographers from airbrushing these out. Our readers want to be able to see what these faces really look like. And they see something they like: a knowing quality, a sense of confidence. It's reassurance that the coming decades are an open door, not a barrier.

Our readers recognize that you can't get that knowing look in your eyes until you're at least 40. Whether you're a stay-at-home mom, a corporate executive, or a schoolteacher, it takes that long to gain the confidence to be who you really are. We find that the bigger we make "40" in our cover headline, whether it's "Life after 40," "Fearless after 40," or "Style after 40," the better the issue sells. We're being very honest about who we are, and about celebrating this stage in a woman's life. And women are drawn to this message.

Aspirations go beyond how we look and style ourselves. We started a new column called "Firsts After Forty," which addresses the strong desire women have to try something new at midlife: to go surfing for the first time, to ride her first motorcycle, to buy her first horse. We featured one woman who went back to college at 40 to become a doctor. People said to her, "You're going to be 50 before you get your M.D." Her response: "I'm going to be 50 anyway, so why not be a physician, too?" Our readers tell us that they feel a sense of urgency: if not now, when?

A big part of this is a commitment to re-inventing their lives. Our readers are undertaking an intense re-evaluation of every choice they've ever made. There's a reason that the divorce rate is rising among women in their 40s. What's more, it's the women who are initiating the splits. They look at their guys and say, "Another twenty-something years with this guy with these same problems? I don't think so."

One of our contributors, Suzanne Brown Levine, author of *Inventing the Rest of Our Lives: Women in Second Adulthood*, addresses the sense that many women feel they want something more in their lives but they're not sure what it is. It's a developmental stage that large numbers of women are just now exploring, and if we can help our readers be patient, the solutions will reveal themselves, bubbling up from their subconscious minds.

We certainly recognize that our magazine is not for every 40+ woman out there. There are subsegments of Baby Boomer women who are less aspirational, less financially well off, less well educated, much more concerned with security, much less likely to set new goals for themselves. There are other magazines for her.

The *More* reader talks about turning 40 or 50 as a commemoration of where she is in life. For her, it's not *"Oh my God! I'm getting old! I have to hide!"* Our readers consider the alternative, grab the surfboard, and celebrate how great it is to be alive.

Peggy Northrop was named editor-in-chief of *More* in April 2004. Under her leadership, *More* made *Advertising Age's* "A List" for 2005, and *Media* magazine named *More* "Best Women's Lifestyle" title of the year. Before joining Meredith Corporation, she was editor of *Organic Style* and held senior positions at *Real Simple, Vogue, Glamour, Redbook,* and *Health.*

Northrop is a regular commentator on CBS's *The Early Show* and PBS's *To the Contrary*.

Brenda Saget Darling was named publisher of *More* in August 2005. She had previously served as publisher of *Traditional Home*. Prior to joining Meredith Corporation, she was vice president/publisher of *House & Garden* at Condé Nast Publications. Her broad publishing experience includes positions at several Condé Nast, Fairchild, and Hachette Filipacchi titles. She also served as associate publisher at *The New Yorker* and *Elle Décor* magazines.

She's Dynamic—Not Invisible

As the chief purchasing officer at home, and having achieved unprecedented success in the workplace, the Baby Boomer woman is anything but invisible. Her life is dynamic, reflecting her continuing development as an individual. This movement provides marketers with fertile opportunities to provide solutions and options for her evolving needs, interests and motivations on multiple fronts. An example of a strategic appeal that does a good job acknowledging this evolutionary dimension of the Baby Boomer woman is created by Dodge. Their print advertisement for Dodge Grand Caravan features a youthful Leading-Edge Baby Boomer woman folding down the seats to make room for her grandkids and their bicycles. The headline reads: "Grab Life by the Horns." Dodge gets it. They have discovered that this generation's Grandma, while happy to be tending to the needs of the younger generation, hasn't given up on her own plans, dreams, and aspirations.

Academia has made note of the unprecedented phenomenon of Baby Boomer women returning to higher education to complete degrees or add degrees to their list of accomplishments. Deborah Natansohn, president and chief operating officer of Seabourn Cruise Line notes a new generation of ambitious travelers, including women, who chart their upcoming journeys five years at a time, checking off regions of the world from their "to-do" lists with business-like precision. And speaking of business, as Maria Coyne of KeyBank points out, an unprecedented number of women, many in the Baby Boomer generation, are following their entrepreneurial dream.

On Banking on Women-Owned Businesses

Maria C. Coyne,

Executive Vice President, Key4Women and SBA

KEYBANK NATIONAL ASSOCIATION

According to the Center for Women's Business Research, the number of women-owned businesses in the United States has expanded by 17 percent between 1997 and 2004, to a total of 10.6 million firms generating $2.5 trillion in sales. At KeyBank, one of the nation's leading financial services companies, we have been committed to women-owned businesses for a very long time. Yet, we realized several years ago that we could better support this growing economic force by dedicating more of our resources to women.

To this end, we launched Key4Women to provide customized service, access to capital, and ongoing education and networking opportunities specifically for women business owners. KeyBank as an organization has made an investment in this segment by pledging to lend $1 billion in business capital to women-owned firms. This, along with our dedicated Key4Women relationship managers in the field, underscores Key's mission of providing a broad variety of services to women business owners.

We believe it's not a one-size-fits-all kind of world, certainly not with the number of women-owned firms out there. It is of great importance to deliver something real, something more than just marketing. We strive to understand the wide variety of women customers we serve and to provide creative and customized business solutions. And we see a broad array of women running business. In fact, many of our more established women business-owner relationships are with the Boomer generation.

We see many Boomer women who are leaving corporate America, starting businesses based on their great work experience. They may have a nest egg or are in a better position to start or buy an existing business. In some instances we see women who, due to death or divorce, suddenly find themselves in a different position and strike out on their own in business.

Much more so than men, women business owners are inclined to consult with others, involving experts, employees, and fellow business owners. According to a study by the Center for Women's Business Research, these women are perfectly willing to be risk-takers, but not before they thoroughly understand how a loan or investment strategy works and determining all of their options. Surprisingly, women business owners, particularly those with firms that generate a million dollars or more in revenues, are more likely than men to embrace technology to help their businesses grow. They utilize their websites to perform more transactions, and their offices are run with greater efficiently using computer networks.

Many women running a business have chosen their path

in part to maintain a level of autonomy and management control in their work. This can mean running anything from a small company with no employees to a large multi-million dollar business with hundreds of employees. As well, we find that women, especially Boomer women, have tremendously loyal staff because they treat their employees like family. This means that often these women will fund a retirement plan even in difficult business years or continue to pay the employer portion of the health care program even when faced with rising health care costs. Of course, the down side of this "family" outlook is that they aren't as quick to make those tough decisions when they must reduce staff.

Given the universal importance women place on relationships and connections, a key element to the success of our Key4Women program rests in the effectiveness and commitment of our relationship managers in the field. We've invested in educating and building awareness with these local champions, for they are the people who bring the whole thing to life. Frankly, many of our Key4Women relationship managers have found it so personally rewarding that the program has become a very strong recruiting tool. Those candidates who are more mature and experienced, and who are looking for something to give them more meaning in their career, really embrace this women-focused initiative. It has helped us to hire some great people. Moreover, Key4Women heightens our commitment to all women. It is changing the way we attract clients and employees and how we service and maintain relationships with an important part of our market.

Maria C. Coyne is executive vice president and national sales manager of Community Banking for KeyBank National Association. Maria is responsible for the national sales efforts and administration of Key's Small Business Administration (SBA) program and leads both Key4Women (women-owned business) and specialty segment initiatives across Key's

13-state branch network. Maria is also a member of the Advisory Council of the Center for Women's Business Research in Washington, D.C. and is the chairperson of the board of directors for the Beaumont School in Cleveland Heights, Ohio.

Outgrowing Old Programming

The revolutionary notion of ongoing adult development is based on the theory that just as there are normal stages of physical development for human beings, so are there normal stages of psychological, emotional, social, and spiritual development. This potential for growth is rooted in the observation that human beings are born with the capacity to experience authentic feelings. However, from the moment the child leaves her mother's womb, she is greeted with frustration and discomfort. Along with physical challenges come messages, influences, and experiences that run counter to her innate sense of herself, programming her with limiting expectations about how things can be. Some women surrender to the limitations, seeking to ground themselves in stability and predictability—even at the expense of their own sense of autonomy and self-expression.

In healthy development, when new information that differs from the original worldview is introduced into the individual's life, she either modifies or replaces the old programming. The old beliefs must be acknowledged as being outdated or dysfunctional in order for the person to advance and grow. This recognition of having outgrown old ways of being is often a painful experience. When it occurs during the teenage years, it's commonly referred to as "adolescent identity crisis." Later in life, this same painful forward movement (that sometimes feels like anything but) has been tagged "midlife crisis." Whenever this crisis occurs, and in many cases, however often, the woman continues her psychosocial development leading ultimately to the reclamation of her capacity to experience, express, and act on her authentic feelings.

The woman's motivational touch-points can be identified and related to one of three major archetypes, each one associated primarily with one of the three stages of development. Before showing you how to apply developmental factors to shape your marketing strategy for your particular product or service, let's dive right in to the motivational archetypes, adapted from the Orsborn/Smull Research.

The Three Archetypes

Archetype One: The Conventional Boomer Woman

The woman described by the first archetype is in a stage of adult development we refer to as Conventional. Her motivational orientation is that of maintaining security, seeking to ground herself in stability and predictability—even at the expense of her own sense of autonomy and self-expression. She has either not been exposed to new information that offers a challenge to the status quo, or she has compliantly resisted any divergent thoughts or behaviors that could be construed as "rocking the boat."

Many women outgrow their original programming in regard to some key life issues relatively early in life, often by late adolescence. A move to a new location, a divorce, education, a traumatic life experience, or any serious challenge to the woman's status quo can initiate awareness of discontent with her limitations. On the other hand, she may be satisfied with her lot and think it more than a fair trade to give up her independence in exchange for the expectation that she will be taken care of by others.

Archetype Two: The Transitional Boomer Woman

At some point in their lives, many women begin to experience the consistent inability to make a decision, the nagging sense that they are being perceived by others differently from how they feel inside, awareness of persistent self-neglect of their physical or emotional needs, and free-floating anxiety. These emotional states indicate that, like it or not, the woman is leaving the Conventional stage and entering Archetype Two, becoming what we refer to as the Transitional Boomer woman. This is the stage during which she becomes disillusioned with what she had previously taken for granted and begins to assert her own individuality.

A woman entering this stage often feels herself to be plunged into insecurity, the old beliefs falling apart while a new, more meaningful world view has not yet come into focus. At the same time old conceptions are passing away, signs of new beliefs and behaviors formed in reaction to them begin to emerge.

In many respects, this vulnerable period bears similarities to an initiatory rite of passage. Social scientists, such as William Bridges and Ronald Grimes, suggest that individuals undergoing transitions at any age go through a similar initiatory sequence, often experienced inwardly as an altered emotional state. In the classic ritual, the initiate is separated from the familiarity of the everyday life of the tribe and put through a series of trials. In the end, transformed by the experience, the initiate re-enters the tribe with the new stature of an adult, having gained valuable skills and insights. While disillusionment is not something most women seek in their lives, it typically heralds a new period of growth.

For example, tired of trying to live up to her fashionable mother's expectations about beauty, one research participant, Samantha, decided to cut her long hair into a crew cut, letting what was left of her mane go a natural gray. But it was equally rebellious of another participant, Joanne, who grew up in an austere fundamentalist household, to not only color her hair but opt for a facelift as well. The key to recognizing a woman in this stage is not so much by her external choices, but by the thought process that she engages in as she makes her decisions. If her motivation has a substantial aspect of reactivity embedded in it, however liberated she may feel or act, she belongs to this second Archetype.

Archetype Three: The Aspirational Boomer Woman

Out of the reactivity of transition emerges the third phase of development, which we refer to as Aspirational. During this culminating stage, the woman moves beyond the passivity of the first stage and the rebellion of the second. The hallmark of the authentic life that arises is integrity: an embrace of opposing tensions, the sum of which constitutes a whole greater than any of the parts. Many women use images of integration to describe their lives in regard to having or gaining meaning: weaving and mending, repairing and healing.

One typical comment from an Aspirational Baby Boomer woman in the study: "Of course I've made mistakes. But that's not the whole story about me. And what's more, it's not even the most important part. I laugh, I cry—and I can finally look people straight in the eye and say 'Here I am, flaws and all'—the whole package. And while I prefer you love me as I am, I am willing to take the consequences."

Said another: "I think of it as the retrieval of lost and broken pieces, patching them together like a broken pot on an archeological dig, making them into something authentic and new."

These Aspirational women know that they are pioneering unmapped territory. Recall that she has three to five decades more of life ahead of her than did her great- or great-great-grandmother at the turn of the last century. The emotional, attitudinal, and practical landmarks she expected to encounter at various ages have quite simply failed to materialize. It is as if the entire generation is simultaneously waking up to the fact that at 40, 50 or 60, they have few role models or historical precedents and no certainty about what the future may bring to draw upon. They may have mixed feelings about dealing with the unknown—but this is a generation of women who are used to forging their own way through history on their own terms.

We are now ready to complete our exploration of motivational influences on the Baby Boomer woman. What is needed at this point is a means of applying what we're discovering about her to your particular marketing strategy.

The Imago Diagnostic

The Imago Diagnostic ("ID") is a tool developed to help marketers identify and surface the motivational profile of your target consumer. There is equal marketing opportunity inherent in each of the three archetypes. As in any analysis, it is important to suspend judgment and avoid assigning positive or negative values to any particular motivational group. The real power of this tool lies in allowing marketers to get beyond the generic age/household income/education parameters to adopt a three-dimensional view of the Baby Boomer woman. By using this motivational model to drive and shape your creative strategy and messaging, you will achieve much deeper levels of authenticity and connection with her.

Figure 4-1 maps the Conventional, Transitional, and Aspirational Boomer woman archetypes. Each of the three archetypes embrace a constellation of internal and external considerations, commonly associated with the equivalent stage of adult development. We view the archetypes through five major lenses, each representing a key area of her life:

- *Work/Life Orientation*: The role work and career hold for her in the context of her life

- *Problem-Solving Outlook*: Her emotional attitude when confronted with adverse circumstances

* *Caretaker/Relationship Mode*: How she approaches relationships and interaction with others

* *Life Stage Impact*: Her views on aging and related issues at midlife and beyond

* *Economic Situation*: Her financial status and outlook

Where would your consumer most likely be located in each of the five categories in Figure 4-1? The outer circle represents the Conventional Archetype. The middle circle represents the reactive, post-Conventional stage of development, the Transitional Archetype. The innermost circle represents the highest level of adult development, the Aspirational Archetype. By referring to the Imago Diagnostic chart, you will be guided toward one of the three archetypes for your consumer.

Given the Baby Boomer woman's capacity for lifelong development, the motivational archetypes we have developed are likewise dynamic in nature. As you refer to the ID chart in Figure 4-1, you will want to keep in mind that the Baby Boomer woman may be at different developmental stages of her life simultaneously. For example, the same woman may have achieved a high level of attitudinal mastery in regards to her career and finances (Aspirational Archetype) while as a new divorcee she is simultaneously coping with the tumultuous emotions of re-entering the singles scene (Transitional Archetype).

To identify your consumer's primary motivational archetype, you will want to place more importance on her Archetypal ID as it relates to the issues or opportunities of greatest pertinence to your company's particular product or service. In the example above, the fact that she is Aspirational rather than Transitional or Conventional in regard to her career and finances will be particularly important information for the marketer of financial products. On the other hand, a company offering dating services will be more interested in

Figure 4-1. The Imago Diagnostic: Identifying motivational archetypes of the Baby Boomer woman.

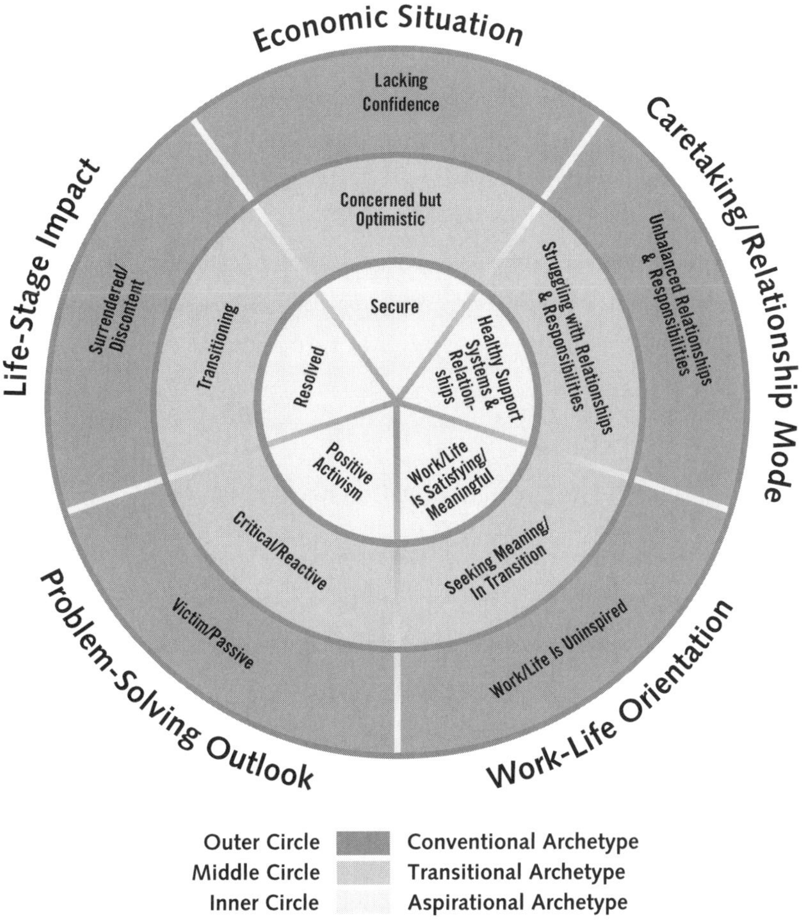

the fact that she embodies the Transitional Archetype in regard to her relationships. At the same time, it is helpful to see her in the bigger picture, offering the marketer degrees of subtlety to build into a distinct motivational consumer ID for her, each with its own messaging, imagery, and appeal.

As with all models, the higher the quality of data you are able to bring to the motivational ID process, the more accurate and complete the resulting ID will be. Draw upon findings from your consumer research, including interviews and focus groups, supported by statistical demographic research as well as industry-specific knowledge to help you make the most informed choices about who your consumer is and what is motivating her.

Motivational Marketing Opportunities

Each archetype carries with it attitudes and characteristics that can help you discern the marketing message that will most appeal to her, as well as the marketing opportunities most closely associated with each type.

The Conventional Boomer Woman

Even more than the other archetypes, the Conventional Boomer woman responds to the voice of authority. Third-person credibility, expert opinion, and statistical justification will all fall on receptive ears.

She is not prone to rewarding herself with luxury purchases or experiences, tending to spend her money on family and friends. When it comes to her brands, she is loyal and conservative.

The consummate caretaker, she puts others' interests first when making a decision. Always keeping family and friends' needs and desires on the radar, she's focused on providing the best solution for those near and dear to her.

She will remain within the Conventional Archetype until she realizes that she has neglected to put one important family member's wishes on the list: her own. The woman to whom this thought occurs is on her way from transiting from Archetype One to Two.

Core Motivational Appeal: *Tell her you can give her the help she needs, and that you will keep her safe.*

Oreck® vacuum cleaners is a company that does a good job appealing to the Conventional Boomer Woman. In a print ad for the Oreck XL® Ultra, David Oreck, dressed in black from turtleneck on down, literally stands behind his product—the Oreck XL Ultra. With his bald head and arms crossed over his chest, he conveys a fatherly yet authoritarian image to his target customer. David Oreck himself is going to take care of all her vacuuming needs, protecting her family. "Hi, I'm David Oreck. It's common knowledge that household dust carries germs, pollen, dander, mold spores, bacteria—things you don't want your family breathing in." Appealing to the Conventional Boomer Woman's low tolerance for risk, the ad does everything it possibly can to lower the bar of entry for her. The company offers eight free tune-ups and an eight-year warranty, as well as a risk-free, 30-day home trial. "There's no obligation. I pay all shipping! Even the phone call is free."

The Transitional Boomer Woman

The woman in this stage is amenable to leaving behind old familiar brands, products and services. She enters a period of open-minded experimentation, rejecting or rethinking purchasing patterns that had become routine to her as she rebels against the status quo. During this transitional period, she begins to pay more attention to her own physical and emotional needs.

An excellent example of a print ad that appeals to the woman transitioning from the Conventional to the Transitional Archetype is for Nature's Bounty's® line of vitamins and nutritional supplements. The ad features an appealing, informal, family-style portrait of a multigenerational grouping of women under the headline: "You Do Your Best for Them, But What About You?"

The woman transitioning from the first to second stages of adult development begins to seek out self-nurturing products, services, and experiences and is open to the self-gifting of luxury goods and experiences.

The Transitional Boomer woman is willing to take risks, to stand apart from the crowd, and to look for ways to individualize her self-expression and life. She is a trendsetter and an early adopter of innovative goods and services.

For example, a Boomer woman travel customer at this stage of growth is likely to respond to a pitch for adventure travel: the solo seeker on a quest for self-definition and nurturing. She is likely to take up a sport or hobby that will raise eyebrows. She is the woman kayaking in New Guinea or training to climb the highest mountain in her state. One thing is for sure: She is no longer concerned about living up to others' expectations. How can you capture this world traveler? You may want to rethink those images of a barely clad couple lolling in the surf. The Boomer woman is just as likely to travel solo, or with her girlfriends, as with a spouse.

Core Motivational Appeal: *Tell her that you believe in her.*

A print ad that captures the spirit of the Transitional Boomer woman is by Vaseline® Intensive Care for Vaseline Total Moisture. The ad features a vivacious woman who appears to be in her 40s, enjoying a good laugh with friends over lunch. Her dark hair brushes her shoulders with lively natural curls and her rose-hued blouse is low-cut to discretely reveal her cleavage. The headline consists of two promises. The first promise: "I promise I'll never get dry skin again." But it's the second promise that provides the tip-off as to her Transitional Stage status. "I promise never to dress like my great-aunt Ethel." Most people wouldn't think twice about the modest display of skin in the photograph. But this Baby Boomer woman's cleavage is apparently an emotionally charged issue for her—as much a sign of her reactivity to the standards by which she was raised as it is her own declaration of independence. In one final huzzah for her, the copy ends on a note of motivational support: "Leave the covering up to great-aunt Ethel."

The Aspirational Boomer Woman

This is the "wise woman" stage. She thinks for herself, but may return to an original brand or product, abandoned during Stage Two, having learned to take a "best of" approach to her lifestyle and consumption choices. She is no longer reactive to the status quo, but knows herself and what she wants. This is a ripe stage to target with products she once enjoyed and used, but that lost her somewhere along the way. She will be responsive to a light touch of nostalgia—but she sees herself as firmly rooted in the present. As a result, she is open to trying new things—but is not likely to sacrifice comfort and practicality for style. Give her both, and you will have a loyal customer.

In the spirit of wholeness, the Aspirational Boomer woman is less obsessed with pleasing others or proving her worth. Rather, she is interested in learning and reconnecting with herself and others.

An example of a motivational appeal to the Aspirational Boomer woman is the January 2006 cover of *More* magazine. In large letters, the cover proclaims "Confident, Grown-up." The subhead reads, "Celebrate Your Life After 40." The featured articles are "Dressy Dresses for Women Not Girls" and "Dream Trips: Finding Yourself in Machu Picchu."

Core Motivational Appeal: *Tell her you will embrace life with her.*

Earlier, we described a print ad in which a Baby Boomer woman sported bifocals (a sign of aging) and torn jeans (the youthful rebel's fashion statement) at the same time. No longer in reactivity to her past, nor in denial about the future, she is finally free to select the "best of" from all her developmental stages and weave them into a way of relating to life that is authentically her own. You might find her deep in yoga meditation one day, going out for pizza with friends on Thanksgiving, and then going whole hog buying Christmas gifts for her extended family a few days later. She's spontaneous and unpredictable, inventing a style all her own.

Saturn appeals to this Aspirational woman with a print ad for the Saturn Relay, commemorating the fact that, "The family car has grown up." In the ad, the attractive Trailing-Edge Boomer woman communicates a hard-won sense of empowerment through the self-confident expression in her eyes. "I am a mother of two, but not just a mother of two. I am more than the sum of my errands," the copy reads. She doesn't deny her circumstance, but at the same time, she doesn't allow her circumstances to define her. Make no mistake, she's her own woman.

Looking for more clues to help you identify key marketing motivators? An expanded version of the Imago ID, titled "A Psycho-Social Inventory of Adult Development for Marketers," appears at www.ImagoCreative.com. The online interactive version, available free to readers of this book, identifies key messaging underlying the psychodynamics of the three Baby Boomer woman archetypes in ten areas:

* Preparing for the future
* Ambition
* Love and relationships
* Parenting grown children
* Unfinished business
* Beauty
* Health
* Inevitabilities (including caregiving, loss, and mortality)

* Creating a legacy
* Meaning

Test your marketing messages against these categories, and you can identify the underlying psychodynamics beneath your (as well as your competitors') communications.

Before we conclude our discussion of motivation, we must take a time out to address two final areas that hold archetypal meaning for Baby Boomer women: The first issue is sexuality, the second issue is the search for meaning.

Seasoned Sexuality

When taking on the stereotypes of aging, what topic is more highly-charged (or more to the point, taboo) for most marketers than the older woman's sexuality? Gail Sheehy, author of the groundbreaking popular work on adult development, *Passages*, faced this stereotype head-on with her publication of *Sex and the Seasoned Woman: Pursuing the Passionate Life*. In this work, Sheehy reports "a surge in women's sex and love lives after 50," tagging the trend "a hidden cultural phenomenon." Sheehy's view is that "Boomer-generation women in midlife are open to sex, love, dating, new dreams, exploring spirituality, and revitalizing their marriages as never before. This is a new universe of passionate, liberated women—married and single—who are unwilling to settle for the stereotypical roles of middle age and are now realizing they don't have to."

This trend toward an extended and in some cases open-ended period of sexual activity in a woman's life is seen by many as an organic adjustment to the elongated lifespan of the individual. With better health and medical advancements that address issues of sexual decline, such as the widespread use of hormones, women have more sexual choices than did their mothers once they entered their postmenopausal years. With the children growing and/or out of the house, many women view this same period in their lives as an opportunity for renewed vitality and passion. Women 40+ are also prime candidates for attempting to start new relationships, populating dating services, and singles bars. (For proof of this, seek no further than ABC on Sunday nights, where four Desperate Housewives set the record straight about their peaking sexuality. In fact, despite the stereotypes, in this age group, it is the woman—more often than the man—who is most likely to initiate a divorce.)[2]

The sophisticated marketer understands that sexuality is not necessarily a thing of the past for her. The Baby Boomer woman will respond to appeals that will help her bring romance back into her life with her husband: exotic vacations, fine wine, sensual lingerie. Alternately, there is the distinct possibility that she could be dating for the first time in twenty-five years. This is a sizable enough segment of the Boomer woman population to have caught the eye of dating services. But even as she goes on the hunt for the best online dating service, body lotions, mouthwashes, and products that promise to give her "kissable" lips, she will not respond to messaging designed with the twenty-something woman in mind.

The reality is, her body is changing. She is not, despite some marketers' conception, buying the notion that she can be "forever young." Nor does she necessarily want it to be that way. Depending on her archetype, she may be anywhere on the spectrum from uneasy denial to whole-hearted acceptance about the realities of aging. In fact, we contend that the sexually-charged woman Gail Sheehy describes is not necessarily the norm, but rather only one healthy expression of the Aspirational Archetype: the woman who is embracing newfound freedoms and loving the body she has.

It needs to be pointed out, however, that this newfound freedom includes the possibility of finding alternative expressions of intimacy and passion that are not necessarily sexually based. As a critique of Sheehy's book in the *New York Times Book Review* reads: ". . . The real subject she's discussing—aging—merits far more depth and attention than even the best vibrator can provide. What about the intangible component called dignity? How to have it, how to keep it, how to teach it?"[3]

The Search for Meaning

Sheehy's conclusion that there is a surge in women's sexuality after 50 came out of her qualitative research, interviewing women across the country. While sexuality did come up from time to time in our far-reaching discussions with women in our study, our research produced a different result. When asked about the topics, issues and/or concerns related to their lives that were top-of-mind, it was the search for meaning that surfaced as the core motivator—the true hidden phenomenon—that underlies all the other categories, even her avowed interest in sexuality.

By "meaning" and "spirituality," we took the participants' implied and/or stated definitions. For the majority, the search for meaning centers around striving for and discovering a more satisfying experience of their lives. For some, this spiritual experience centered around traditional concepts of God, as transmitted through organized religion. For others, spirituality was a diffuse (or in some cases, distinct) sense of being part of something beyond physical reality that is larger than themselves. This search for meaning can inspire the Baby Boomer woman to seek out experiences, communities, products, and services that hold the promise of feeding her yearning for something more.

On Her Quest for a Free Spirit

Federico Musi,

Vice President of Marketing (Piaggio, Vespa, Moto Guzzi)

PIAGGIO GROUP AMERICAS

The woman on a Vespa scooter is the image of sexy sophistication, form and function coming together on the streets of London, Paris, and New York. She's a chef, an editor, a new condo owner—and more likely than not, she's middle-aged!

Vespa, introduced to the marketplace in 1946, turned 60 the very same year that the Leading-Edge women of the Baby Boomer generation celebrated their 60th birthdays. People may be surprised to hear that Boomers represent 40 percent of the Vespa market, with women representing a large share of this segment.

She sees a Vespa as a reward for all that she's accomplished. After years of delayed gratification, parenting, working hard, and taking care of others, she's ready to explore new dimensions of life. Now she's on a quest, fulfilling lifelong desires such as traveling, writing, and spirituality. She is, in fact, expressing her full power.

It should come as no surprise that such a large segment of Vespa owners are Baby Boomer women. After all, this is a woman who has the disposable income, the independence, and the desire to appreciate what Vespa has to offer. In terms of form and function, Vespa has been an iconic brand since day one. It was originally designed to solve the transportation issues in Italy in the wake of World War II. With gas at a premium, the scooter was relied upon to get the man in the business suit, the woman in a skirt and the priest in his gown from place to place, as efficiently as possible. Vespa was not conceived as an upscale product, removed from the masses, but designed for the people. In Italy, Vespa is part of everyday life, with moms and grandmas among the crowd who routinely take the scooter to shop, commute, or take the kids to school.

In America, there is an added emotional appeal that goes beyond the ordinary. Going against the norm of women driving cars, the woman in America who buys and rides a Vespa is celebrating her independence. Moreover, she is communicating the message that she is a sophisticated woman who appreciates beautiful things, elegant simplicity, and a balance between responsibilities and freedom. At the same time, to appeal to her, the product has to offer a practical benefit. For her, saving gas—both for budgeting and environmental reasons—has appeal, as does the premium but not inaccessible entry level of $3,200.

In terms of marketing to her, Vespa has several challenges. While Vespa is a leading manufacturer of scooters in the world, the U.S. scooter market is still in its infancy. We need to gradually educate the market on the benefits of scootering and attract those early users that will become our most faithful brand and product ambassadors. Alternative marketing channels, such as PR, product placement, and local events, are at this stage more effective then traditional advertising. Happily, we find Baby Boomer women are very receptive to these channels. Actors riding a scooter on a television program or in a movie, or celebrity chefs jumping around town between restaurants, help us connect to our target and fuel that aspirational drive for the viewer to buy one for herself.

One of the latest and most innovative ways we connect with her are via several of our blog sites, hosted by women who are passionate about Vespa. The female "host" of the Vespa Quest blog site leads the visitor through the process of buying her first Vespa scooter, from researching the product to getting a license, going through the process online. Women identify with her quest, bringing a spiritual dimension to the act of buying a Vespa.

We are also pursuing innovative partner marketing. For example, we're going after condo marketers with the idea of having them include a Vespa in the condo purchase package. This provides them with an edge in a crowded condo market, such as South Florida. Wouldn't you prefer that condo pictured with a Vespa in the driveway?

Federico Musi served as a senior consultant at McKinsey & Company in both the Milan and New York offices, prior to his joining Piaggio USA. His client work focused on several industries, including financial services, media, and retail. His expertise includes corporate and business unit strategy, sales and marketing, and organization. Before joining McKinsey, Musi worked as a project manager for the oil giant ENI. He received a master's degree in engineering from Padova University (Italy) and an MBA from Columbia Business School. He currently lives in New York City with his family.

Increasing with Age

Many of the women in the study reported having expected that as they aged, the most they could hope for was acceptance of their increasing powerlessness and a graceful fading away. However, for many of these women, their reality is turning out to be far different. Rather than the serene acceptance dictated by the stereotypes of aging, the majority of the women reported themselves to be in dynamic states of transition and development. Among Transitional and Aspirational Boomers, we noted their generally optimistic view.

Even when facing the toughest challenges related to aging, their expectations in regard to what they often reported as being most important to them—a sense of meaning—was, in truth, increasing with age. Even the Conventional Boomer woman expressed the desire for meaning in their lives, fueling the rising numbers of church attendance in large part by women in this archetypal segment.

Far from buying into the belief that their power is destined to diminish as they age, the majority of Baby Boomer women are shedding the old stereotypes, coming to view time as the means of actualizing their true potential. More and more of this generation of women are tapping into their ever-growing reservoir of self-knowledge, external resources, and communal wisdom. As one of the Transitional Boomer women in the research study summarized: "Given everything that's been happening in my life lately, I have the suspicion that spiritual proficiency can no longer be considered a luxury."

CHAPTER FIVE

She's in the Driver's Seat

She'll Problem-Solve Her Own Way Through the Marketplace

Over the course of the last several chapters, we've been unraveling the myth of the existence of a "stereotypical" Boomer woman. While it is essential to speak to her diversity, there is one unifying factor that should nevertheless always be kept front-of-mind, regardless of all the other qualifiers that come into play. She is, above all, a woman.

His and Her Marketing

As we mentioned earlier, men and women are wired differently. He prefers the big picture and broad strokes, using a more linear and logical approach to making decisions. Her decision-making process, on the other hand, takes a layered and cyclical path, where subtlety, details, research, and word-of-mouth play influential roles (see Figure 5-1).

Understanding these key gender differences, as they relate to communication, problem solving and the purchasing process, affects the development of marketing messages, products, and services that successfully "speak" to her.

While men and women go through similar phases in regards to the consumer decision-making process, the relative importance of each individual phase, the tactics utilized to move through the phases, the factors influencing the decisions made during each phase and the amount of time invested differs greatly.

While the purchasing process we are about to describe can apply to women generally, many of the qualities and characteristics described by this model are more pronounced for the Baby Boomer woman.[1] For instance, while most women are turned off by hype,

Figure 5-1. Understand and speak her language.

SHE	HE
• Views group interrelationships as communal.	• Perceives group interrelationships as hierarchical.
• Connects via empathy.	• Defaults to competitive exchange.
• Views people and relationships as the most important element in a situation.	• Values autonomy, independence, and concrete actions and accomplishments.
• Thrives on multitasking (but craves simplicity), thinks contextually and holistically.	• Moves through tasks methodically and sequentially, likes facts, figures, and stats.
• Tunes into subtle inconsistencies, details, and peripheral environment.	• Focuses more on the big picture.
• Physiologically, displays greater interconnected activity between brain cells and across the left (logical) and right (intuitive) sides of the brain.	• Physiologically, has a larger, more dominant left side of the brain, the area responsible for analytical, linear processing.

this more seasoned woman's purchase decisions are even less likely to be swayed by gimmicks and hyperbole. Having grown to maturity in an era that spans the one-on-one, simpler purchase environment of their youth to the highly technical, mass-market landscape of the twenty-first century, Boomer women are the most highly developed and demanding consumers in the marketplace today.

How the Baby Boomer Woman Shops

Phase 1: Need/Problem Recognition

As the primary purchasing officer and caretaker of just about everything and everyone, she is "problem recognition" command central. Even if she doesn't personally need that acne medication, hair-loss formula, or incontinence panty, she's got her constituent's needs (in this case, teenage son, husband, and mother-in-law) front and center of her mind. A man, on the other hand, tends to recognize need as it arises and pertains to his realm.

Phase 2: Search for Information

The Baby Boomer woman's search is all encompassing, more lengthy, and nonlinear in its progression. In terms of the decision-making process, men are hunters and women are gatherers. As a true "gatherer," she will start by reaching out to all referents for an opinion and enlist the knowledge of her network. Her first choice of contact is personal interaction; if not an actual warm body, then a telephone customer rep, a brochure, or a website that anticipates her questions and multiple levels of needs. Her search is driven by finding not just a solution, but the ultimate solution.

On the other hand, a man, the hunter, goes direct to the source: examining the actual product on his own or referring to the trade magazine or consumer report site that he's relied on for years. He wastes little time, and zeros in on getting to the heart of the facts and features. In contrast to a woman, he is not driven to "complicate" the search process; this only adds time to getting the darn thing crossed off his "to-do" list.

Phase 3: Evaluation of Alternatives

When considering alternatives, she will place higher value on benefits versus features. Does it solve a problem or better yet, multiple problems? Is it simple and superior? Is it aesthetically appealing, and does it reflect her self-image? She will also more stringently evaluate the perceived value of incremental investments in additional features.

As a contextual and experiential being, the Boomer woman brings all her senses to the evaluation process. Sounds, smells, lighting, textures, and colors—all register with her. She may love your product, but that pulsing techno-beat over the speakers, or that price tag so tiny she can't read the numbers, will drive her away.

As household chief purchasing agent, she may enter into negotiation with her "constituents" during this time of evaluation. Does the cruise she has in mind appeal to her husband? No putting course on board? Well then, she's back to the research phase.

Men evaluate and eliminate alternatives in a single-minded fashion, based on logic, features, power, and what the product says about their knowledge and taste. The innate male tendency to operate autonomously and independently means less consulting with referents or constituents to slow down his process.

Phase 4: Choice/Purchase Decision

For her, the search is for the ultimate solution, not just an adequate solution. Even when she has finally selected a product she'd like to purchase, the transaction may not be ready to be consummated. The value-conscious Baby Boomer woman may decide to wait for a sale or special promotional offer that she suspects is coming. Just because she didn't make the purchase today, don't write her off, for she could merely be circling around her decision, searching for that last key detail to tip the scale. She's savvy to the ways of marketers and will make the company work for the sale.

Men on the other hand, go for the kill and begin consuming their product immediately. They rarely wait for a sale when their need is pressing. In fact, they will more readily pay a premium for express shipping.

Phase 5: Post-Purchase Evaluation

Given her drive for the ultimate solution, after the purchase she is still looking for confirmation that she made the right choice in solving her initial need. She wants to know your company appreciates and values the relationship she has begun or chosen to continue, albeit on her terms. How you handle the post-purchase experience will be key in fostering her trust and future involvement with your brand.

Men spend far less time, if any, in this phase. Driven less by relationships, spending time getting to know you after the fact is not their priority.

On Getting to the Heart of the Matter

Joe Teno,

President

ATHLETA

For the best clues on how to relate to today's Baby Boomers we should go way back to when they were babies, or at least when they were learning their way in the world. What values did they adopt? What made them comfortable? What made them happy?

Let me tell you about my friend Maria. She grew up in Medford, Massachusetts. In 1969, Maria was 15 years old. She lived with her parents and her grandparents in a single family, three-story house. The house occupied a small lot and everything that wasn't paved was turned into a vegetable garden. Maria's grandmother had a green thumb and insisted on growing almost everything they ate. Their house was filled with the most inviting, appetizing smells one could imagine. In the summer, pots were always simmering on the stove. Some were dedicated to canning tomatoes; some were turning tomatoes into irresistible "gravy," as Maria's mom referred to it.

For a few hours each day Maria worked at the corner store. It wasn't the prepackaged, self-serve, 24-hour convenience store we are used to today. Maria had to grind hamburger, scoop ice cream, and "jerk" the soda fountain to get the syrup and carbonated water to mix properly. While she was doing this, Maria carried on a conversation with the customer on any number of topics. She didn't have a script; she was just being herself.

When Maria was invited to the senior prom she had a great shopping experience. Early on a Saturday morning, she and her mom boarded the bus, connected with the train at Sullivan Square, got off at Washington Street and walked to Filene's. Maria's Aunt Rita worked in the teen department and, although Maria didn't know it, Maria's mom and aunt had been planning this expedition since Maria got the invitation.

Aunt Rita, smiling and excited, had already sorted through all the prom dresses and put the best ones aside for Maria.

She showed Maria each one, talking about the fabric, the sewing, where it was made, and how the colors matched Maria's skin and hair. They settled on a light blue, full-length dress with crisscrossed straps. Maria was the first in her family to go to college, and she remembers vividly the celebrations the family gave her when she graduated from college and then law school.

The 1960s weren't perfect. There were no computers, e-mail, voice mail, cell phones, fax machines, beepers, or even answering machines. Nevertheless, when you called a business or even dialed zero on the rotary dial phone, you were connected with a live person immediately.

Fast forward to 2006. Maria is now 52. Consciously or unconsciously, what do you think are important elements in Maria's shopping experiences? She has a fine eye for detail. Quality is paramount to her. Maria likes to be "known" and appreciated when she shops. She likes relationships. She doesn't demand perfection; she made mistakes in the corner store, but when she did she offered a heartfelt apology and it usually went a long way. Any purchase, especially a big one, is an event, and when a salesperson treats it that way it always adds to her experience. Sure she loves a bargain, but she's not at all reserved about paying a premium for a unique product. Maria even shops with a few companies that offer loyalty programs. She remembers Green Stamps and the water glasses her father brought home whenever he got a full tank of gas. Above all, Maria notices and appreciates great service.

Where does marketing fit into this? Specifically, how does one market to the female Baby Boomer? For starters try substituting "intelligent, mature, and confident" for "Baby Boomer woman." Beyond that, I'm not sure these women want to be "marketed" to.

She's interested in a relationship with a company that offers unique, high quality products that are a good value. She expects the same service, connection, and relationships she may have experienced 35 years ago: an engaged, knowledgeable sales person who knows the product and takes pride in pleasing customers. She wants to deal with companies that exhibit character and integrity, always. She wants to know that you treat your employees and the environment with care. She wants to be recognized and treated respectfully.

Nothing magic. And certainly nothing new.

Joe Teno is president of Athleta, a catalog and Internet retailer specializing in women's active apparel. After receiving a master's degree in business, Joe started his catalog career in 1984 at L.L. Bean. Over the years he has gained hands-on experience in almost every facet of the industry. When Joe isn't working he's training for or participating in various sporting events. To date, he's completed seven running marathons and two cross-country ski marathons. Joe lives with his wife Gail in Petaluma, California.

The linear approach that a man typically takes through the decision-making process, versus the layered and complex path embarked upon by a woman, can be visually summarized in Figure 5-2.

Again, the male tends to move through tasks methodically, satisfied with finding a good solution. She, on the other hand, incorporates new information all along the way, revisits her decisions, and cycles back around again in search of the ultimate solution.

Figure 5-2. Purchasing process by gender.

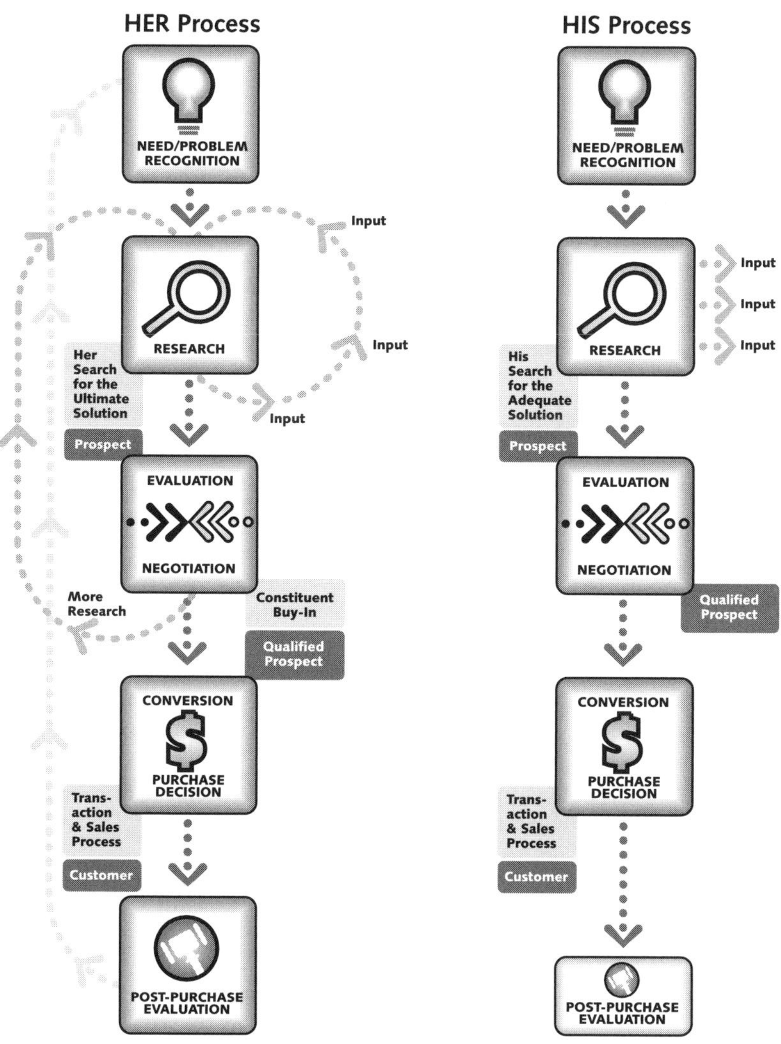

Focusing on the "Why" vs. the "How"

Heidi Baker,
Chief Jane Officer

Eden Jarrin,
Chief Executive Officer

BE JANE, INC.

We started Be Jane as a branded media company to provide content, community, products and services for the women's Do-It-Yourself (DIY) market. Through BeJane.com and our television, print, radio, and online partners, we are putting a public face on women's home improvement and creating a trusted and credible information source for female homeowners everywhere. As the founding "Janes," we launched Be Jane in response to our less than supportive personal experiences within the home improvement industry, and the realization that the women's home improvement market was highly fragmented. There was no one source women could turn to for community, support and relatable DIY information.

Our community on BeJane.com embraces a wide variety of women, each with a unique story, experiencing a different life stage, and armed with varying DIY skills. Their biggest commonality is their desire to be able to take control of their home and home environment, becoming a "do-it-herselfer" in a male-dominated home improvement market. The majority of our community is comprised of women Boomers and beyond—married, divorced, widowed, and in many cases, responsible for their own home for the first time in their life.

Currently women spend $50 billion a year in the home improvement industry which is a relatively new phenomenon, and has left many wondering why this market is growing at such a rapid rate. We believe that media is a major influencer of perceptions, which is why we launched Be Jane as a multi-platform branded media company. In the recent past we've seen an increase in cable channels that base their entire programming on the topic of home improvement, such as HGTV and the DIY networks. The disconnect we found was the lack of support available for these women to actually implement what they saw on TV in their own reality. The women of the Boomer generation, who typically had been taught to rely on the "man of the house" or end up at the mercy of a contractor, are now starting to feel a certain amount of control and empowerment through taking care of their own home improvement needs.

"How to" information is not a new concept, so why haven't women just read the many "how to" books on the market or taken a weekend class at a local home improvement center? Well, many women have tried the resources available to them and came into contact with either a fear of being able to actually accomplish the project at hand, or a lack of motivation and support needed to take on more extensive projects. In addition to creating a resource that "speaks" to women, Be Jane also approaches home improvement from a different point of view. We focus more on the "Why To" of a project than on the "How To." Our members have shown us that women tend to respond more positively when they can first focus on the end results of a project as opposed to the mechanical aspects of how to accomplish it. We emphasize the overall change it will make in their lives such as making their bedroom more romantic, or their kitchen more functional. Once the end result becomes visible, the process of completing the "how to" becomes more relatable, worthwhile, and satisfying.

Be Jane also helps women navigate the rigors of home improvement by communicating the realities of success and failure. Many of our members express their fears of failing in doing home improvement projects. We not only address this issue, but we also provide them with the tools to get past it. After all, women are not necessarily more confident now; they are just more willing to try something new. Our members may start off timid in their project choices but after one success their confidence begins to build and the subsequent projects become increasingly more difficult and the rewards become greater. We tell our community that the hardest part of doing a project is doing it for the first time—and the easiest part is doing it a second time. To diminish the fear even further, we share stories of women of varying ages and ethnicities: how they succeeded, how they failed, and most importantly, how they managed to solve problems that arose along the way.

If there is one thing we've learned it's that women inspire women. An interesting finding though was that younger women are particularly inspired by the accomplishments of older women. For example, we have women in their 70s taking on ambitious home improvement projects for themselves and their grandchildren, consequently inspiring a whole generation of younger first-time homebuyers. The strong response we've received from our members makes us believe that marketing campaigns with this type of focus on the inspiration and wisdom of mature women would be successful in other parallel industries.

Heidi Baker and Eden Jarrin, The Janes, are cofounders of Be Jane, Inc., the first branded media company and online resource dedicated to women's home improvement. Founded in 2003, Be Jane was born out of Heidi and Eden's own experiences and passion for empowering others. Together, The Janes are dedicated to educating, inspiring, and equipping women with the knowledge and tools they need to have confidence in home improvement and themselves. As a former purchasing agent and now Chief Jane, Heidi leads Be Jane's content, branding and product development. As a previous founding team member of a NASDAQ traded company, Eden is CEO and oversees Be Jane's core strategy, Web, and strategic partnerships.

Transparent Marketing

Many marketers worry that by designing campaigns that take the Boomer woman's needs seriously, they risk alienating other consumer segments, most notably men and younger women. Several of our contributing marketing experts admitted that they held this concern initially. Yet, to their surprise, they discovered that by accommodating the more complex needs of their Boomer women consumers, they ended up designing products or services that won over men, as well. As Amy Marentic of Ford Motor Company points out: "Ironically, when we set out to please the woman, adding the features she asked for such as extra cup holders, places to store a bag or briefcase, and the command seating, it appealed to the man in her life, as well. He might be thinking about transporting golf clubs, more so than his in-law's wheelchair, but by pleasing the woman in the buying equation, we get the man as well."

Here's another example, taken from the world of high-tech. By creating a PDA with more intuitive controls, more legible numbers, text and buttons, shaping the product ergonomically to be more easily grasped in the hand, and offering the product in colors other than black, your product will rank higher on the Boomer woman's list when she's considering her PDA purchase options. At the same time, younger generations of consumers will appreciate these enhancements, as well.

Hilton Garden Inn chose a transparent approach in their print ad strategy, satisfying her desire for details, while simultaneously prioritizing the key service likely to sway him. Overlaying a photograph of a tasteful, light-filled Garden Inn lobby are half a dozen shaded text boxes listing multiple amenities, such as "Amenity 36: Breakfast buffet & evening room service. Amenity 48: 24-hour Pavilion Pantry® with everything you forgot. Amenity 34: A well-equipped exercise room to offset Amenity 36. . . ." Given that the Boomer woman traveler wants to know as much as possible about her accommodations before she books a reservation, by listing all these services Hilton sends the message that they understand what she needs. Realizing that guys are less interested in the fine print, the ad's headline, "We'll obsess about your stay . . . You obsess about your game," coupled with a larger, highlighted "Amenity 18: Complimentary golf," Hilton also delivers on the one most relevant amenity for him.

Overt Marketing

Transparency, however, is not always the best solution. No doubt, some products and services demand an overt gender/generational targeted strategy in order to make the most resonant connection. Marriott's Courtyard went with a dual-gender print advertising campaign, creating separate ads for their female and male consumers. Her ad, with the headline, "Log on and on . . . ," shows a female executive, sipping tea in her pajamas, e-mailing family and colleagues from the comfort of an overstuffed chair in her hotel room.

His ad, headlined ". . . Road warriors designed our [hotels]," exhibits a male executive getting dressed in business attire, manning control-central at his technology laden in-room business center. Whether transparent or overt in your strategy, deeply understanding and identifying the unique drivers of your target segment is paramount.

Winning Her Loyalty

Regardless of whether you take a transparent, hybrid, or overt approach to win the attention and loyalty of the Baby Boomer woman, you have to show her that you understand and take seriously her purchasing-process characteristics and core values. To succeed with her, you will not only have to build her values into your advertising campaign and communications materials, but into the heart of your marketing initiative. There are eight main deliverables to keep in mind.

Eight Main Deliverables

1. Help Her Solve a Problem
2. Provide Her with Genuine Value
3. Offer Her Customization
4. Promise and Deliver on Authenticity
5. Provide Her with Filtering Tools
6. Feed Her Attention to Details
7. Satisfy Her Demand for Service
8. Humanize the Experience

1. *Help Her Solve a Problem:* Above all else, this is a generation of women who historically let nothing get in their way—for long. Now they are turning their problem-solving skills towards the issues of

aging, defying the stereotypes both individually and as a group. The marketer who helps her problem-solve her way through these new challenges life is bringing her way is the marketer who will win her loyalty.

2. *Provide Her Genuine Value:* For Boomer women, genuine value is not just about price, but is a more complex cocktail. Ira Mayer of EPM Communications suggests that, "Companies should create value for their women customers by delivering compelling content, establishing emotional resonance in their messages, offering time savings, being convenient, providing entertainment, improving her experience, and being economically superior."

3. *Offer Her Customization:* Brands that create a process of discovery drive passion and ownership of the brand. Baby Boomer women like being in the role of creative director, feeling that they are driving the shaping of the products and brand. Born from her generation's focus on the individual and the desire to differentiate herself from the mass market, this trend toward customization will continue to grow with the flexibility and efficiencies offered by technology and in manufacturing.

Consider Land's End Custom™ jeans, and how she can design pants individually tailored to her body shape and style preference and have them delivered to her door in two weeks. Likewise, Lab21 takes customization to new heights by creating individually formulated skin-care products based on one's DNA. Customers take an at-home DNA test and answer a questionnaire about the health of their skin. LAB21's SkinProfiler System then creates a custom formula (with the customer's name on the label) to treat specific conditions.

On the Personal Shopper Approach to Technology

Melissa McVicker,

Director, Global Communications Group

INTEL

The key to acceptance among Baby Boomer women is to show them that technology can provide solutions tailored to their own particular needs and challenges.

As Intel is gathering information on the Baby Boomer woman's buying patterns, one thing we've learned about this discerning generation is how important it is to provide them with personalized choices. When you think of targeting her needs, think personal shopper as opposed to one size fits all. For instance, with the advent of the lighter laptop PC, women no longer need to be confined to the ugly black computer bag. Instead, they are converting bags made for other purposes, such as diaper bags and totes, and transforming their cases into personal fashion statements. Intel has worked with a European designer to create a PC bag for laptops with Intel® Centrino® mobile technology specifically with women in mind.

The Asian high-tech market is years ahead of the United States, catering to the special needs and interests of both women and the older population. In Japan, for instance, a woman can purchase a cell phone tailored to her own particular interests or needs. Her passion may be entertainment, such as a Hello Kitty-themed phone. Or it may be physical, such as a phone with extra large numbers for aging eyes. In

Hong Kong, a woman can even buy a phone that allows her to keep track of her hormonal cycle.

Another aspect of technology that is of particular interest to Baby Boomer women is the potential of cutting-edge nano-technology to forge new frontiers in consumer electronics, and even in a multiplicity of bio-medical applications. Professionals and prevention-minded consumers alike will be able to access the most recently updated patient charts from a hand-held device as healthcare goes digital. These developing aspects of technology are of particular interest to the health-conscious generation of Baby Boomer women, particularly as they age.

Keep in mind that women tend to turn to products that create or enhance their life experience. For instance, a Boomer myself when I went on my sabbatical from Intel to the beaches of Bali, I played with the notion of leaving my PC behind. The last thing I wanted was something that reminded me of work. Then, I realized that my laptop could actually enhance my experience by helping me stay connected with family and friends and find helpful information while traveling within Bali. Happily, I decided to bring it along, downloading my digital photos to communicate with the people back home while sitting on the beach. I was able to research travel options while I was there, and connect up to real people who had opinions about quality of service at restaurants and hotels, and so on. This real-time use of my computer while on vacation capped the months I'd already spent online in a state of vicarious anticipation as I planned out the trip in the first place.

Some high-tech companies will be better at capturing the attention of the Baby Boomer woman than others. As a whole, lightweight laptop products are where we see the greatest progress in making online time a portable, life-enriching and aesthetically appealing experience for the Baby Boomer woman. But this is only the beginning.

As sales of lightweight laptops go through the roof, it has become increasingly clear that tech consumers are no longer predominantly tech-savvy, 18- to 34-year-old men. The fact is that the majority of Internet users are not young men, but women. As an important part of this segment, the Baby Boomer woman is being increasingly viewed by the high-tech industry as a serious customer for consumer electronics of all kinds.

Melissa McVicker is responsible for managing Intel's communications strategy and worldwide media and industry analyst relations as part of Intel's sales and marketing organization. Previously, she spent over three years based in Asia Pacific, as a regional marketing manager. Prior to that, McVicker worked at Compaq Computer Corporation, HP, and various start-up companies in marketing roles. She earned her bachelor's degree in electrical engineering from the University of New Mexico and MBA in marketing from UCLA's Anderson School of Management.

4. *Promise and Deliver on Authenticity:* Rykä started twenty years ago as a brand catering "solely" to women's fitness shoe needs. Taking into account women's narrower heel and wider forefoot, Rykä designs shoes on a woman's form. But they go beyond their tagline of, "Inspired by women for women" with a corporate commitment to women's initiatives like Avon's Walk for Breast Cancer, sponsorships of the women's only *More* Marathon, and the Rykä Women's Fitness Grant Program. Rykä also partners with Curves and Lady Footlocker to encourage women's fitness through product discounts. Rykä has grown with their female consumer, expanding into sporting apparel for women's needs in running/walking and circuit training and studio fitness. Rykä's print campaign follows their theme line: "Inspiration. Build right in," and shows a light blue fitness pullover, half-constructed of inspiring photographs of women

engaging in life and active pursuits. This ad taps into women's aspirational and emotional needs, connecting on a level that is perceived as authentic.

With a streak of idealism running through the core of this generation of women, brands must cultivate authenticity on a level never demanded before. These women are smart, resourceful, and savvy. If your brand doesn't deliver on all its promises, or fails to speak to a consumer's specific, personal needs, your brand will become irrelevant.

Further, the Baby Boomer woman expects your company to behave authentically and demonstrate an active alignment with the values you claim to embrace. Simply slapping a pink ribbon on your website will no longer cut it. And with the oversaturated celebrity endorsements for every cause imaginable at an all-time high, her skepticism of gratuitous posturing by brands is on the rise. She's more likely to do business with brands committed to corporate citizenship and good causes that are aligned with her values. If your company supports a cause, ethnic and gender diversity, mentoring, or community and environmental involvement, make this information readily available through your marketing channels.

5. *Provide Her with Filtering Tools:* Today's Boomer woman, especially the Trailing-Edge "club sandwich" contingent, juggling career, kids still at home, and aging parents, has created her own chaotic and harried life by insisting on fulfilling everyone's expectations and maximizing every opportunity. She is often driven to give 100 percent to every task.

In our info-saturated, hyper-speed lives, time is the new currency. Barraged by more information than we can ever hope to absorb, we have what retail-shopping guru Paco Underhill refers to as a "process crisis"—how do we get the wisdom out of all the data with the least amount of time investment?

Consumers look to companies, media, and marketers to provide information filters—tools to edit mass amounts of data in the time available. As Robyn Waters, former vice president of Trend, Design and Product Development for Target, points out, "Too much information without editing is toxic." Give her the tools to organize, search, and access product information in a way that is efficient and relevant to her needs.

Search engine marketing has evolved as a vital component of harnessing the power of delivering filtered information when and how she wants it. But to effectively filter and communicate relevant data to a consumer, marketing and creative directors need to be well-versed in the art and science of interpreting, translating, and delivering information. This requires generational, gender, cultural, and ethnic expertise as well as sophisticated global knowledge of word associations and linguistics. The information we have shared with you in the previous chapters gives you a leg up on this, when it comes to the Baby Boomer woman.

One company who has done an excellent job filtering and communicating relevant data to specific consumers is Amazon.com. Its highly developed preferences filtering keeps track of the individual's interests, making recommendations based on her ever-growing profile, providing product reviews, updating daily a customized list of the newest and coolest products customers are buying—essentially creating a personal shopper to save the consumer time. And it does all this in six different languages with the appropriate cultural insights for each.

6. *Feed Her Attention to Details:* For her, the devil is in the details. It's the little things that can make a big difference. From sales brochures and websites to retail environment and customer service, she will notice and expect details and quality nuances much more than men.

On Paying Attention to Details

Kathy Moyer Dragon,

Founder

THE DRAGON'S PATH
ACTIVEWOMEN.COM

I have spent the last two decades of my life designing, marketing, selling, and leading active vacations for women to places around the world. Over the years I have personally led approximately 3000 people on small group biking, walking, trekking, snowshoeing, multi-sport and cultural trips, family trips, and student programs.

Many of the women on these trips have become personal friends and have traveled with me multiple times over the years. On each of these adventures we spend the better part of 16 hours a day together and often for nine to twenty-one days at a time.

With these women I have shared life's transitions: the dilemma of being single and not wanting to be; dating, marriage, children, divorce, death and illness of children, husbands, parents; 40th, 50th, 60th birthdays; their concerns about growing older and the expectations of staying younger; the search for passion and fulfillment in work, relationships, and all parts of life; the fear of failure and the overwhelming excitement of accomplishing a goal . . . especially one that could not have been imagined twenty years earlier.

When you spend such intense time moving about unfamiliar and often uncomfortable areas of the world with a group of women, you talk about everything (and laugh a lot). Think about it . . . from shuttle services to parking, airports to airlines, hotels to restaurants, boots, packs, scarves, moisturizer, socks, makeup, cameras, telephones and carriers. Nothing is "usual." This is the beauty of travel. Going out in the evening, with a small set of clothes to choose from, becomes a creative fashion show with a captive audience.

One of the most important things that I have learned from the active Boomer women I have traveled with is that women notice the details—before anyone else—whether it is appreciating the quality of a towel or discussing the variety of cultural opportunities of a particular day trip.

When the travel brochure arrives in the mail, they notice how the envelope was addressed. Was it addressed to *Mr. and Mrs.*, when there is no Mr.? Was it handwritten or mass mailed? Was there a personal note for returning clients? They notice the feel of the paper and if it was printed on recycled stock, the emotional impact of the imagery, and the size of the font (often it's too small for bifocaled Boomers).

When they call or e-mail the company, they care how the phone was answered (hopefully directly by a real person). They want to talk to someone who listens to them and asks question, calms their fears, encourages them, speaks informatively. In general they don't want fifteen itineraries to choose from in Tuscany or Nepal. They want three to four that are clearly different for specific reasons (e.g., classic route, more remote/cultural, boutique properties, or comfortable camping).

Because of their busy schedules and lives, they want programs offered in modules (nine-day core trip with a two- to three-day pre-city escape, post-jungle option, etc.) so they can choose what fits their interest and availability.

When they receive the confirmation materials, the destination information and packing list is extremely important. They want the packing list to be as specific as possible with recommended brands as well as descriptions on what it will be used for. They read all the "cultural" details of what is and is not appropriate and safe in the area.

Once on the trip, the first few days are most important. Staying on schedule, the social aspect of introductions and putting anxieties to rest are all key. The first day they want assistance in fitting packs, checking footwear, and reminders to drink water.

Small luxuries are important: offering simple things like hot water and mini-spa treatments on a trek, impromptu pre-dinner happy hour gatherings, and assisted shopping adventures; purchasing foreign stamps in advance; offering massages when possible; and assisting with little details that will make her experience more comfortable while still keeping it an adventure.

After the tour, Boomer women are busy. The importance of a big trip to them can be life changing. Once the "group" is created, a new community is formed. No one at home will be able to share or understand what has transpired on the trip. Keeping these relationships going by way of a yearly calendar, mini get-away reunions, shared photo sites, and e-mail lists enhances the group's commitment to each other and maintains your connection to her.

Kathy Moyer Dragon, a twenty-year veteran of the adventure travel industry, brings a unique perspective to the past and future of active travel. Having strategically designed and marketed numerous adventure travel packages, Kathy has shaped and guided the experiences of over 3000 guests. Of these small group adventure and cultural trips around the globe, two-thirds of guests are Boomer women. Kathy has been instrumental in the growth of niche companies including Vermont Country Cyclers, Country Walkers, and Whole Journeys. She has a reputation within the adventure travel market as a trusted leader in all aspects of the industry.

7. *Satisfy Her Demand for Service:* Customer service is not a unique message—everyone claims to give great customer service. However,

only 19 percent of women say they actually receive good customer service even though 97 percent expect it.[2] What if your brand really did deliver on customer service along with other value indicators?

On Business "Plus"

Anne Kelly,

President

JUNONIA

I started Junonia in 1995 because I was simply a Boomer in the gym, noticing how many of us were there, and that a good share of us wore a size greater than 14. I was probably early to the plus-size issue, but certainly it is the story of the day now!

The Baby Boom woman is smart and wants to be treated that way. Moreover, she wants to know that this dedication to service goes to the very top of the company. We think it's important to cultivate a one-on-one relationship with our customer. For that reason, there's a photo of me right on the home page, and an e-mail link that allows the customer to communicate directly with me. This direct contact between president and shopper means that our customers can become deeply involved in guiding the clothing styles that Junonia might offer down the road—and it means that there is a strong, personal loyalty that goes both ways.

We try to stay very practical. Our customers appreciate our respectful, active, and healthy approach to plus-size apparel that is reflected in our catalog images. But after that, they just want merchandise that is high quality and in stock when they order, a website that is quick and easy, and customer service people that can help them make great purchases.

In conjunction with our catalog, our customers get frequent e-mails from us, and we always try to ask ourselves what would make her value this next marketing approach. Sometimes it's a gift, a discount, or some information about leading an active life. We don't always get it right, but we keep looking for those win-win-wins. We know when we get it right, she will send that e-mail to all her friends, and therefore the circle expands.

Anne Kelly is the founder and president of Junonia, a catalog and Internet retailer of women's active clothing. She founded Junonia in 1995 to serve the sports and fashion needs of women who wear a size 14 and up. The Minnesota-based company has used the Web extensively, being named one of the "Top 50 Websites in 2005" by *Internet Retailer* magazine. Anne has a master's degree in business management from the London Business School.

8. *Humanize Her Experience:* The mind-bending advancements of the Web and computer technology have thrown life into warp speed. From an evolutionary standpoint, technology has infiltrated every aspect of our lives faster than we can assimilate the changes. Though women in their 40s and 50s are far more comfortable with technology than those over 60, the Internet and high-tech gadgets have only been an integral part of Boomer women's lives for the last decade or so. In contrast, her Gen X and Gen Y counterparts can barely imagine a world that is not tech-centric.

You will want to create a comfort zone for these women by "humanizing" any technology associated with your product or utilized in your marketing communications. Deliver a brand experience where the technology is transparent to her. Products, services, and communications fashioned around innate human behavior, instead of the ideals of a programmer, will win her.

Hewlett-Packard leads the pack with their "you + HP" consumer brand campaign, focused on taking the hassle out of digital photography. Visually fun, full of creative energy and real life scenarios, their ads devote minimal space to showing actual product. Instead they go to the heart of image-making—documenting, sharing, and making memories. HP touts their digital cameras and printers as, "radically simple picture-making technology, which lets you be in control of the entire picture-making process." They back up their claim with easy-to-navigate, thorough online product support.

A great example of a product that is getting it right in all of the above seven categories is Apple's iPod™. Compelling content is delivered via their Web portal, allowing the consumer to download a free single of the week, digital liner notes, and even video clips. Emotional resonance is created using hip messaging and visuals that subtly infer how the iPod relates into your life. For example: "Music Is the New Black," "Enjoy Uncertainty," and "Picture Your Music." The iPod and companion iTunes offer consumers time savings and convenience by eliminating the need to go to the music store only to find out that the Sting CD that was just released is not available. On iTunes, you can download it within seconds. The iPod provides entertainment by allowing you to create and share custom playlists and essentially become a closet DJ. It improves your experience because it helps eliminate clutter (no more CD cases with mismatched CD's inside) and makes your entire music library portable. Most importantly, it's economically superior because the iPod can multi-purpose itself for use in your car, at your computer, in your house, or even while you're exercising.

Once you have these key loyalty builders in place, you are ready to connect to her. Next: what channels of communication will work best with her?

CHAPTER SIX

She's Changing Channels

Shaping the New Brandscape

In Chapter One, we asked you to imagine walking into your local news stand and seeing photographs of women 40+ on the covers of national magazines. By now, you recognize how rare it is for the Baby Boomer woman to be featured in mainstream media. But just because the woman over 40 has not been given her rightful due by the mainstream media *yet*, doesn't mean she's mute or invisible—if you know where to look and listen.

The fact is that women of the Baby Boomer generation are powerfully connected and communicating to one another through a vast personal, professional, social, and spiritual network of tributaries. For example, on any given day, month, or year, certain consumer-generated e-mails that resonate with her can be counted on to be making their way to her inbox. Be it a funny or inspirational line from a poem, a summons to visit a particular website to donate clicks for free mammograms for needy women, or a warning about an inferior product, service, or experience (merited or not), the rate and reach of these communications matches the effectiveness of the most successful multilevel marketing pyramid schemes—without the prospect of diminishing returns.

These messages travel around the world and back again in the click of a mouse, 24/7. Online forums, too, such as www.BoomerWomenSpeak.com, are literally visited by millions of women with no ulterior motive on anyone's part other than to connect into the generational Zeitgeist when in the mood for community. This affinity for relationships and networking are core elements of the Baby Boomer woman's DNA, and when she comes together with like-minded women, watch out! Anything is possible.

Relationships Rule

There is incredible potential inherent for marketers in engaging with, nurturing, and supporting her networks and relationships. When a product, service, or cause that hits a nerve with her is adopted within these groups, the impact can be enormous. One reason that many marketers have not yet recognized or figured out how to tap into her "networks" is that many of these networks fly beneath the radar of mainstream marketing channels. In this chapter we bring specific examples of these evolving channels to light.

We begin by addressing the impact of the marginalization of women over 40 from the media mainstream on the women themselves. Remember from our discussion in Chapter Five, she is hungry for authentic relationships; she is energetic; and she is engaged. Above all, she is a problem solver. If the mainstream media ignores her or doesn't give her what she wants, she'll make her own way. It is helpful to think of her as a river of intention, flowing around the obstacles, between the rocks and over the waterfalls—even going underground, if necessary—on her way to the communal ocean where the richness of relationship she craves awaits.

Some companies have done a good job, plunging into the ocean with her, discovering just how fast they need to swim to stay afloat. For example, have you been into a major chain bookstore lately and noticed a new category of books? We're not talking biography or travel. Rather, we draw your attention to a growing collection of literature gathered into its own special section for members of "The Red Hat Society." Unless you are a woman 50+, you may well have walked right by, without even noticing that a segment of the population has become so powerful as to merit their own special section of the bookstore. Now that we've pointed this out to you, begin paying attention to the presence of red hats in your environment. Go into gift shops in the "ladies-who-lunch" part of town, some antique stores, or even at higher-end truck stops, and you will see racks of red hats, as well as sparkly red hat pins and dazzling t-shirts. You may see a gaggle of women in red hats out to dinner together. You may happen to look down and notice the Red Hat licensed sneakers on her feet (Grasshoppers® by Keds), the official Red Hat Society glasses encrusted with Swarovski crystals perched on her nose and lipstick designed exclusively for The Red Hat Society (with matching nail polish) on her lips and nails.

What is this Red Hat Society—or more to the point, what is the implication for marketers? The Red Hat Society was "inadvertently" founded in the late 1990s by Sue Ellen Cooper of Fullerton, California, when she and a few friends took inspiration from a popular poem that celebrates finally becoming old enough to get away with wearing a red hat and purple dress. Sue and a few friends began meeting on a regular basis for tea, suitably attired. Word-of-mouth, accelerated by editorial and articles in the press, quickly spread around the world. By 2006, The Red Hat Society had attracted more than a million members, spawning thousands of chapters across the United States and thirty countries, including Australia, Mexico,

Japan, and Egypt. Exalted "Queen Mother" Sue Ellen Cooper reaches more than 90,000 Red Hatters each week through a Friday broadcast, a personal e-mail updating members on society happenings. Consisting primarily of women 50+ who are drawn to the organization for its "social interaction, fun, and friendships," members include working women, grandmothers, retirees, golfers, attorneys, and teachers as well as women who are widowed, married, and single.

The Red Hat Society presents a prime marketing opportunity for companies who want to reach a large number of women of the Baby Boomer generation. In fact, The Red Hat Society has agreements with more than 30 companies to offer services as well as licensed merchandise online and at select retail stores.

Match the Organizational Archetype

However, before choosing to align your brand with any organization, remember that Baby Boomer women are a diverse lot. One of the differentiators is the variety of roles she plays in regards to her relationship to the status quo. Recalling our motivational archetypes, she may fall anywhere on the spectrum from compliance with the status quo (Conventional) or outright rebellion (Transitional) to living life on her own terms (Aspirational).

Taking The Red Hat Society as an example, it is important to note that within the Baby Boomer generation, there are women who are drawn to the energy of this particular group—incorporating it into the very core of their identity. There are others who join in on occasion, just for fun. Then, too, there are Baby Boomer women who not only do not identify with the Red Hatters but who are, in fact, embarrassed by grown women dressing up in what they perceive to be costumes. They fear that women over 50, who are willing to act and look silly, feed the stereotypes that older women are not meant to be taken seriously, reinforcing their potential for marginalization from the mainstream of societal power.

The savvy marketer will want to make sure that the archetype of their consumer is in sync with the organizational persona of any marketing partnership candidate before diving in.

Grassroots Growth

Another spontaneously generating network with a distinct persona that has swept through Boomer women circles over the past few years is the hit show "Menopause the Musical®," a production featuring Baby Boomer women performing re-lyricized tunes from the 1960s and 1970s. Addressing the issues and challenges of aging while saluting women who are experiencing "The Change," the show has played in over forty cities around the United States and in countries around the world. Each week nearly 30,000 women attend the show, with an estimated 6 million having been in the audience since the show's opening in Orlando in 2001. Building on the show's success, there is now an associated magazine, expos, and foundation. The possibilities for marketers include everything from lobby rack cards and booth space at the expo, to sponsor links from the "Menopause the Musical" website, and inclusion in their print and electronic media ads. Their grassroots promotional literature distribution channels provide access to such hands-on communications venues as Curves Fitness Center, OB-GYN offices, and mammography centers.

Nonprofit and charitable organizations also have the potential to harness the strength of women who come together in affinity groups and networks.

On Harnessing the Power of Women's Solidarity

Adam Hicks,
Vice President, Marketing and Communications
CARE

Over the past several years, CARE (Cooperative for Assistance and Relief Everywhere, Inc.), known for it's post-World War II "CARE Package" program, has been addressing the increasingly complex challenge of keeping our brand relevant in the global fight against poverty. We've taken a closer look at what field strategies are the most effective in dealing with the root causes, not just the symptoms, of poverty.

We've discovered that the success of our programs is directly attributable to nurturing women's empowerment. In helping the women of poor communities, whether by enabling small business startups, confronting the spread of HIV, or providing education for their children, we create agents of real and lasting change.

As marketers, we search for that compelling truth about our product and then connect that to an audience to whom that truth is going to matter. We realized that a natural constituency for fundraising and advocacy for CARE—the audience who most cares about empowering women—is logically women 35+ in the United States.

Women of the Baby Boomer generation know what it feels like to be marginalized. They too want to realize their own dignity. This generation of women is more in touch with that experience than younger women in the United

States. Also, with age comes the desire to understand one's place in the world and make a difference. As well, women 35+ simply have more money and resources to contribute to our cause.

But we really hit a bull's eye when we decided to drill even deeper within the women 35+ demographic and harness the power of women's affinity groups. By virtue of having already joined a professional or civic association or church group, there's a strong chance that she already believes in women's empowerment—that when women come together good things can happen to her and good things can happen to other women in this group. Our marketing campaign, with the tag line, "She has the power to change her world. You have the power to help her do it," resonates with this target audience and in turn connects the target audience back to meaningful ways to engage and help women in the developing world.

From a marketing standpoint, we are looking to take people on as short a journey as possible to get them to take action and get involved in CARE. By working through women's networks and affinity groups—connecting their existing belief in women's empowerment to women in the developing world—we've made that trip much easier.

Adam Hicks has been vice president of marketing and communications for CARE USA since 2000. In that capacity, he led CARE's first ever global re-branding initiative, course corrected declines in the size of CARE's donor base, and co-created strategies that have grown CARE's private revenues by an annual average of 18% over the last five years. Prior to joining CARE, Mr. Hicks spent 12 years in customer, channel and consumer marketing at The Coca-Cola Company. In his last four years there, Mr. Hicks was director of the Global Education Market Development and in that capacity, spearheaded efforts in over 60 countries around the world. Mr. Hicks began his career with the NCR Corporation.

Traditional Woman-to-Woman Networks

Not all the networking success stories are grassroots phenomena. Take for example the direct-selling industry, which has experienced an unprecedented nineteen consecutive years of growth. Woman-to-woman networking is fueled predominately by college-educated Baby Boomer women selling products to one another via one-on-one or group gatherings in the comfort of each other's homes.[1]

A successful new arrival on the scene is Tastefully Simple, ranked number 44 in *Inc.* magazine's 500 fastest growing privately held companies,[2] offering upscale, easy-to-prepare gourmet foods sold via tasting parties. One up-and-comer in the do-it-yourself arena is Tomboy Tools, with its popular Tool Parties, where women can get in-home demonstrations of their products in action. And last but not least, there are the pioneers of the woman-to-woman marketing channel, enduring veteran brands such as Avon, Tupperware, and Mary Kay cosmetics.

On Real Women Selling to Real Women

Yvonne Saliba Pendleton,

Director of Corporate Heritage and Corporate Communication

MARY KAY, INC.

Mary Kay, Inc. has always recognized the importance of Baby Boomer women—America's largest demographic—who account for half of all consumer spending. The cosmetic company's appeal is one that Boomers embrace—both with its direct selling career opportunity and with its products.

One of the key strengths of Mary Kay's appeal is that "real women," instead of celebrities, are its stars. Within the giant independent sales force, there is an innate respect for those women who blazed trails and opened doors for subsequent generations. This admiration is, in fact, a powerful symbol that is not lost on the Baby Boomer generation.

With its highly successful anti-aging products, Mary Kay® is a brand that Baby Boomer women have come to trust and to recommend to their daughters and granddaughters. In all its marketing vehicles, the company has stayed away from images that stereotype any age group or demographic, preferring instead to represent women of all ages and backgrounds. Its communications clearly articulate the benefits and features of products—especially those targeting the anti-aging benefits and their accompanying scientific studies.

Even though Mary Kay has brands and products that are specifically meant to appeal to the younger Gen X and Gen Y customers, the stalwarts in its respected skin care regimen have definite appeal to Baby Boomers. Mary Kay has always helped Boomer women feel special and shown them the respect they deserve as they age—albeit gracefully and with their ever important self-esteem intact.

Mary Kay Ash employed her "thinking like a woman" business philosophy from the very early days of the company, and that thinking has continued alongside the amazing growth of women-owned businesses. According to the Center for Women's Business Research, there are over 10 million women-owned businesses in the United States, generating $2.5 trillion in annual revenue. Women are starting businesses at nearly twice the rate of men, and some credit leaders like Mary Kay Ash with making that trend possible.

Without question, the Baby Boomer woman demographic is a vital segment of Mary Kay's target audience, and success with these consumers will continue to increase as more products are developed that cater to this group. This demographic presents the beauty industry with what is truly a tremendous opportunity for expansion for companies like Mary Kay, who've not only embraced this segment, but who are more than willing to address its ongoing needs.

Yvonne Saliba Pendleton, director of corporate heritage and corporate communication for Mary Kay, Inc., is an award-winning journalist and former newspaper editor in the Times Mirror and Newhouse organizations. She's the author of three books, and was instrumental in several best sellers during her tenure at Mary Kay. A Baby Boomer herself, Yvonne has lived the legacy of her generation from her early 20s in Dallas, when she was named the nation's youngest fashion editor for a major daily newspaper.

The Influencer Revolution

The need to establish a personal relationship with the Baby Boomer woman is occurring in industries across the board. What is happening with her, in fact, is no less than a consumer-driven revolution, with the traditional hierarchy of communications vehicles literally turned upside down. We refer to this as "The Influencer Revolution," illustrated in Figure 6-1.

As Figure 6-1 illustrates, the traditional marketing hierarchy was a top-down model, with authorities—such as media experts, academics, scientists, celebrities, political and business leaders—carrying the most weight with consumers. The marketing message that used to work best for them was, "We know. Listen to us." Their authority was transmitted downwards through a mix of marketing channels, including traditional print and broadcast advertising, sales force activity, sales promotion, direct marketing, telemarketing, and out-of-doors.

Figure 6-1. The influencer revolution.

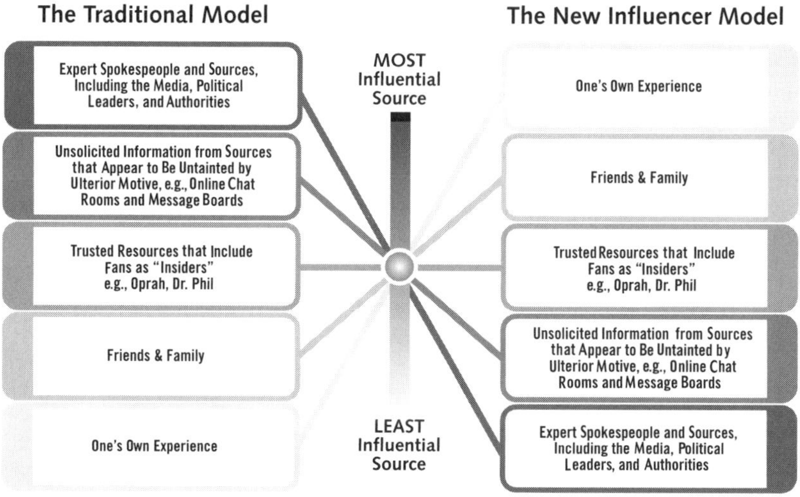

While the Conventional Baby Boomer woman still responds to this message, the majority of women have grown beyond the authoritarian appeal. In the new upside-down influencer hierarchy, the majority of consumers are no longer at the effect of the message—the recipient of the communications from above. For Baby Boomer women in both the Transitional and Aspirational Archetypes—comprising the majority of the demographic on most marketer's radar screens—it is the consumer herself who is calling the shots in terms of what information she is seeking and who she will allow to get through to her. This does not mean that she is no longer receptive to the opinions of public personalities, as witnessed by the tremendous clout of Oprah, Dr. Phil, and even Donald Trump. However, for an authority to make a positive impact on the Baby Boomer woman, the expert must be able to establish a relationship with her, treating the fan base as "insiders."

This sense of "chatting among friends" explains the success of the television shopping channels, talk shows like "The View," and programming that creates the opportunity for interactive involvement with the consumer. Even Oprah, always on the leading edge of marketing trends, has made sure not to let this one slip by her. Every day, after her daily talk show program, she now has her "Oprah After the Show" venue, inviting her special friends to hang around and chat unscripted and unrehearsed—the ultimate perk for Oprah's self-selecting insiders. Authorities who lack the charisma of presumed intimacy do not enjoy the same ability to influence the Baby Boomer woman.

Word-of-Mouth

Given her relationship-orientation, the Baby Boomer woman places more credibility on word-of-mouth information than any other marketing channel. In fact, in recognition of its effectiveness, "word-of-mouth" has become a legitimate new kid on the marketing channel block, promoted and professionalized by new marketing organizations such as WOMMA (Word-of-Mouth Marketing Association). Since word-of-mouth recommendations usually come in the form of stories or personal anecdotes, they tend to be more memorable. Additionally, they have the advantage of being more transferable from woman-to-woman than traditional advertising or sales messages. Above all, there is the appearance of objectivity: the promise of accessing an authentic opinion, untainted by ulterior motives.

Deborah Natansohn of Seabourn Cruise Line points out that an unsolicited recommendation from a friend bears more weight than the expert travel writer's opinion in a guide book or magazine.

On Referential Not Deferential Marketing

Deborah Natansohn,
President and Chief Operating Officer

SEABOURN CRUISE LINE

More than any other sector of the travel industry, the cruise industry succeeded in reinventing itself during the last decade of the twentieth century. A major factor in this is the maturing of the Baby Boomer generation: the most affluent, best traveled generation in history. The Baby Boomer woman, who is the chief vacation planner for her family, doesn't make her travel decision deferring to guide books or magazine articles. She tends to be referential rather than deferential, relying on word-of-mouth recommendation from the people in her life she knows and trusts. She will go on an Internet bulletin board and listen to other Baby Boomers talk candidly about their travel experiences rather than believe what the experts say in a magazine. Word-of-mouth is key for us, and we have referral programs that we offer to our guests, providing them with a benefit for encouraging their friends to try one of our cruises.

Our biggest source of business is still the travel agent, however, who has built a relationship with her customer on our behalf. For the agents, it creates an annuity, because they know if they sell a Seabourn product, that person will come back to them over and over again. One travel agent recently told me that, in fact, she never just talks about one vacation with her affluent clientele. Rather, she does the travel equivalent of a business plan, helping her client map out where she wants to go and with whom she will be traveling over the next five years.

Baby Boomers view vacations as a God-given right. They would never think of denying themselves a vacation unless they were in dire economic need. Even middle-income Boomers are less self-conscious about self indulgence than were their parents. In fact, Baby Boomers have changed the definition of what even an entry-level luxury product is. Boomers have become used to a certain lifestyle in their homes, work, and urban environments. In today's competitive market, the luxury traveler knows that the sheets are going to be of the finest cotton, the food is going to be prepared by a well-known chef, and there's going to be Wi-Fi accessibility.

To earn the reputation of being the best in the world—to justify the luxury price—you've got to sell more than the facts. When the consumer is purchasing a luxury product, she is looking for an evocative experience, not merely a list of destinations and features. For example, Seabourn's cruise in the Mediterranean isn't wonderful simply because it goes to Venice, Florence, and Rome. Instead, we convey to her that when sailing into Venice on a Seabourn ship, she'll have the opportunity to take a gondola ride on the Grand Canal, one of the most romantic things to do in the entire world.

What motivates the Baby Boomer woman is more the "soft"ware than the hardware. This year, we instituted a personal shopper program. If you know you're heading for Istanbul, and you want to shop for antiques, we'll arrange to have someone who has expertise in that area take you shopping for the day.

This difference between software and hardware is illustrated by the marketing launch of the Queen Mary II that I led for Cunard. With Cunard investing $800 million in this ship, they understandably wanted to see a picture of the ship in their ads. But strategically, I felt that the hardware was not what was going to sell the dream, the romance, and the experience of a transatlantic crossing to our target Baby Boomer market. Instead of the ship, our ad campaign portrayed women engaged in everyday situations, such as feeding breakfast to the family, reading in bed with their husbands, and unloading groceries from the car. However, in each of these scenarios, the woman was dressed in an elegant ball gown. The headline simply read, "Can you wait?"

The campaign received a great deal of attention. But most importantly, we filled the ship. I came away from this campaign affirmed that the best approach to marketing to our Baby Boomer woman is to help her realize that she does, indeed, deserve a luxury experience that will fulfill her desires, needs, and fantasies. And then, deliver on the hope.

Deborah L. Natansohn was appointed president of Seabourn Cruise Line in July of 2004, with a mission to guide the ultra luxury cruise operator through a major reorganization that would create a separate company within the Carnival Corporation family of cruise brands. Prior to Seabourn, Natansohn joined Cunard Line in November 2000, where she was responsible for all marketing and sales programs throughout the Americas, including the immensely successful introduction of the new flagship Queen Mary II. A well-known travel industry veteran, she also served as president of Orient Lines, breaking the glass ceiling to become the first female president of a cruise line in the United States.

Extending the Reach

As a natural extension of word-of-mouth, many companies are finding that adding subject-matter specific forums or chat rooms to their websites feeds this generation of women's hunger for both information and relationship. Such conversations, even on a corporate-sponsored site, are perceived by consumers as providing less biased information than editorial copy on the same site. Marketers are finding ways to connect with pleased clients, and encouraging them to share their satisfaction with friends and peers via referral incentives, online reviews, and testimonials. At the same time, as some are less happily discovering, if she has a bad experience with you, she'll talk about it even more.

Product placement also continues to be an important influencer, although the most effective contexts for product visibility are those in which the utilization of the product appears to be natural and organic. The best placement of all is the unsolicited endorsement by influential customers who hold sway over their network of relationships. Rick Lovett of H2O Wear discusses how influential it is when the teacher of a water aerobics class is wearing one of H2O Wear's chlorine-resistant bathing suits while leading class.

On Delivering Beyond Expectations

Rick Lovett,

President

H2O WEAR

When I purchased H2O Wear over a decade ago, its primary market was youth swim teams. However, taking note of increased participation in aquatic activities among emerging markets, I decided to shift the company's focus. A key market for us, and one that continues to hold out future potential, is the Baby Boomer woman. As the active Boomer generation matures, many are increasingly turning to the pool for a challenging yet rewarding workout. Many of these women who have turned to water exercise just can't take the pounding of floor aerobics anymore. For larger woman, exercising in water takes the weight off their knees. Water therapy, too, is being prescribed as good for arthritis and other physical conditions where low or no impact exercise is mandatory.

As these women find themselves spending a significant amount of time in the pool, they are increasingly looking for suits that not only fit their changing body shape, but a quality product that won't fall apart after a short period of time.

"I am your company's worst nightmare," are the exact words I recently heard come from the mouth of one of H2O Wear's valued customers.

She went on to explain that she had purchased one of our ChloroGuard suits years ago, and still wears it in the pool on a regular basis. The quality of the material and manufacturing were so high that she had yet the need to go out and purchase another bathing suit.

After listening to her share her experience, I responded by saying that actually, she wasn't our worst nightmare. To how many people had she told that exact same story, I asked. She paused for a brief moment, looked at me, and nodded her head in understanding.

At H2O Wear, we believe that the longer our product lasts, the better. Our customer base is one which gravitates towards quality and value. As a result, we don't get much price resistance, but instead we receive tremendous word-of-mouth. We have never set out to be the low-cost company, but have focused our efforts to manufacture a high-quality product. By delivering more than what the consumer expects on all fronts, we have established a community of brand stewards, spreading our message of durability and comfort. We then reinforce this exposure with print ads and catalog distribution.

H2O Wear takes a unique approach to raising awareness of our product. Instead of increasing our volume solely by growing our catalog list, we attempt to capture groups of people rather than individuals. We seek out the places where potential customers congregate, such as fitness clubs, public pools, and aquatic therapy centers. This is a demographic that enjoys the social aspect of exercising. Before long, she's not one of twenty strangers splashing around together in the pool. Friendships develop, and these women love to share their opinions. It has been this type of extensive word-of-mouth exposure that has transformed the company into what it is today.

Knowing that the public perceives aqua instructors as knowledgeable and trustworthy leaders, we first educate these instructors on our product line. They then indirectly form a brand connection with our target market, the participants. "Perceived Knowledge Leader" is the person who has a certain role and is therefore held in high regard to know the most about an industry and its products. An example in our case is the notion that aqua aerobics instructors know of the highest quality bathing suit, and it is most likely the brand they are wearing themselves.

By educating and establishing strong relations with the leaders in our target market, the instructors bring our brand directly into the consumer's life. So, first we convince a select few to try our product, and then we educate them on what distinguishes us from competitors. Lastly, and most importantly, we consistently deliver beyond the customer's expectations. We have found this formula successfully produces not only positive word-of-mouth, but brand loyalty as well.

Rick Lovett purchased Wilton, N.H.-based H2O Wear in 1994. Since then Lovett and his management team have transformed the company from a catalog retailer of team swimwear to a catalog and Web retailer of women's swimwear that caters largely to women over 50 years old. Prior to acquiring H2O Wear, Lovett was a vice president of commercial lending at Bank of Boston. He graduated from Ithaca College with a BS in Business Administration.

The Changing Role of Public Relations

The importance of public relations in the marketing mix has grown dramatically over the past several years, as its role in word-of-mouth, buzz-generating publicity, and promotional strategies has become increasingly important to marketers making the effort to connect with women of the Baby Boomer generation.

An example of a public relations campaign that aggressively targets women 35+ is Proctor & Gamble's Crest brand. Promoting its new Crest Whitestrips Renewal tooth whiteners, P&G needed to make a big entry into the anti-aging category. The campaign they created centers around the theme line: "Keep them guessing." In addition to TV, print, and online campaigns, the PR effort aims to get "real people" modeling their own natural smiles. Crest has launched a micro-site, KeepThemGuessing.com. Consumer pairs who defy stereotypes of aging, such as mothers and daughters who look more like sisters than different generations, are invited to enter their photos into an online gallery to win various prizes. The website also offers interactive games, coupons, and educational information about the product.

A related nontraditional marketing strategy that holds strong appeal for Baby Boomer women is the incorporation of an educational element into the core of the marketing outreach. Stonyfield Farm®, makers of all-natural, organic yogurt products, places little emphasis on traditional advertising vehicles. Rather, they rely on educational opportunities to grow their customer base and generate brand loyalty.

"At Stonyfield, we focus on building awareness and educating more people on the benefits of organic," explains Stonyfield Farm's vice president of communications, Cathleen Toomey. The company communicates with their target market through their website, blogs, package lid program, community involvement, and educational summits. "We've built the company over the years on word-of-mouth, increasing brand loyalty."

One of the cornerstones of the Stonyfield marketing effort is their sponsorship of the Stonyfield Farm *Strong Women* summit retreats, featuring Dr. Miriam Nelson. Dr. Nelson's seven best selling books, under the *Strong Women* title, have sold millions of copies around the world and launched a grassroots movement of women supporting women to live healthier lives. Open to women of all ages, the summits hold particular appeal to Boomer women, who respond to Stonyfield's offer for an opportunity to learn ways to be healthier physically, mentally, and spiritually. The Stonyfield Farm summits have multiple corporate sponsors, including GlaxoSmithKline and Newman's Own.

This relationship-building strategy cements brand loyalty and strengthens Stonyfield Farm's network of customers. By delivering an experience rather than just a product, Stonyfield Farm transforms these customers into brand evangelists, who take it upon themselves to generate positive buzz for the brand.

However popular attendance at in-person events like the summits may be, the potential to leverage the relationship-building aspects of educational initiatives by taking them online reaches geometric numbers of consumers. When you visit Stonyfield.com, you enter a thriving online community. From their daily blogs providing information on organic industry news, e-coupon offers, and recipes, you learn not only about the company, but are also educated on a variety of organic food topics.

But it doesn't end there. A visit to the site yields directions to a page dedicated to "Strong Women." Through the virtual summit portal, the consumer is led to a photo album of attendees at past summits, "5 Tips for Staying Strong," "10,000 Steps for Better Health," "Recipes for Strength," and a forum feature where visitors are invited to "discuss strong women."

Perceived as a trusted resource, Stonyfield Farm empowers their consumers to be brand stewards who spread their message and merchandise.

The Influence of the Internet

Much of the influencer revolution is attributed to the impact of the World Wide Web. Certainly, the Web and Baby Boomer women have evolved into a marriage made, if not in heaven, at least in cyberspace. Even though the Web was created as an internal communications tool for the U.S. Defense Department, it has evolved into the perfect channel to connect all aspects of the Baby Boomer woman's multitasking, busy life. It is vitally important for marketers to understand her use of the Internet in light of her relational DNA.

As previously stated, for the busy Baby Boomer woman, time, more so than money, is the new currency. As her personal tool, the Internet allows her to take full advantage of those unpredictable free moments between tasks. She can maintain her personal as well as professional relationships over time and distance. (Because of this unprecedented ability to stay connected online, an "Old Girl's Network" has kicked in at last, rivaling Old Boy's Networks in its ability to keep Baby Boomer women tapped into high-level career opportunities. Here is one instance where having lived a lot of years, and probably having changed positions numerous times, possibly living in various parts of the country or abroad, pays off with rich and deep networking possibilities.) As her primary means of research and management, the Internet provides her access to the resources and information she wants and needs, when and how she wishes to receive it.

On Staying Relevant for the Boomer Woman

Ed Kinney,

Vice President, Corporate Affairs and Brand Awareness

MARRIOTT VACATION CLUB INTERNATIONAL

Our industry has had ten consecutive years of 20+ percentage growth. Not only is our industry fast-paced and expanding, but so are the channels and strategies of communication that we are using to target and sell to purchasers. For instance, three years ago, we were selling $650,000 a month off the Internet. We're doing about $6 million a month off the Internet now. Given the explosive growth and changes in our industry, Marriott has had to essentially reinvent itself every four to five years.

Families are our general target audience, yet we recognize the female within that segment is an influencing decision maker. One dynamic area of growth for us is the segment we refer to as "Grand Boomers": Baby Boomers, not necessarily retired, who want to share the Marriott vacation experience with their adult children and grandchildren. These Boomers are at the peak of their earning potential. Additionally, as this generation is maturing, they are increasingly motivated by the desire to leave a legacy to their families. We've positioned timeshare ownership as a solution that allows Boomers to spend quality time with their families, enjoying what they've worked hard for, while knowing that their families can enjoy the timeshare for generations to come. As an example, one of our owners recently bought nine weeks at her timeshare—one week for each child and grandchild, deeded in each child's name.

Technology has significantly enhanced our ability to capture ongoing data that helps to understand the evolving needs of customers as they navigate life stages. Without being obtrusive, we are able to learn from our customers' buying patterns and tailor products, promotions and marketing messages to specifically meet their interests. In this way, our timeshare product stays relevant as the Boomer's vacation and family dynamics alter.

For example, if a current owner purchased a property ten years ago, when their child was in elementary school, we know that their child is now in their early twenties, probably getting out of college and establishing their own adult lives. We can assume that the owner no longer has the cost of tuition while having more discretionary travel time, and will probably want to be adding new destinations tailored to their new life stage. They may now want to add an experiential resort to their portfolio, such as Palm Springs or Hawaii, that features an atmosphere geared more to personal enrichment instead of activities with their young kids.

Timeshare ownership is still a face-to-face purchasing experience for the most part. What has changed is what happens prior to the actual purchase. Prospective buyers use our website in the research gathering stage of the purchasing process. Now, by the time they get to the face-to-face meeting, their level of knowledge and interest in the product is much higher than it was five or ten years ago.

Truly understanding what the Baby Boomer woman's needs are, what she is searching for, and how we can connect with her are all keys to Marriott's growth in the timeshare industry. What has also been essential is one step beyond that: not only delivering on expectations, but anticipating what customers will want next as their lives, and their families, evolve.

Ed Kinney oversees all public relations for Marriott Vacation Club, Horizons, Grand Residences by Marriott, and The Ritz-Carlton Club brands. In his sixteen years with Marriott Vacation Club International, Ed has also served as director of field marketing and senior director of brand advertising and communications. Prior to Marriott, Ed was a principal in the Idea Factory, an advertising agency focused on fractional resort development properties. Ed is currently the chairman of the American Resort Development Association Public Relations Committee and committee chairperson of the Central Florida Marriott Business Council.

Developing the Online Experience

As marketers become savvier about how to effectively connect to her online, the Internet's role in the marketing relationship with her is only going to get bigger. Because of its importance, we have specific advice for marketers who want to offer her an online experience that will turn the Baby Boomer woman into a loyal customer.

Following are seven things you need to consider when developing a Web presence that will successfully connect with the Baby Boomer woman.

It's a Boomer Woman's World (Wide Web)

1. Get Past the First Date

Baby Boomer women are looking for ways to enhance and simplify their lives, all while staying connected and informed. As we said in Chapter Three, when she's online, she's looking for fast and easy access to relevant information, services, and products. She knows exactly what she's looking for, searching the Web efficiently—viewing 40 percent fewer Web pages than men.[3] When she achieves her goal, she's on to the next task. Give her what she wants and she'll be back, the highest compliment not necessarily how much she purchases today, but that she bookmarks your site and becomes a regular visitor.

Don't underestimate the power, positive or negative, of your Web presence: 30 percent of women say that a bad website will not only induce them to shop somewhere else online, but also can make them less likely to buy from that same company offline.[4] Her favorite sites are thoughtfully planned and simply designed. Almost 65 percent of women rate good design and ease-of-use as extremely or very important qualities in a website.[5]

2. Let Her Drive the Technology, Not Vice Versa

In addition to learning everything you can about her motivations and needs, you've got to scope out the level of sophistication with which she is apt to engage with your technology, as well.

For example, as of 2005, the Nike Women site was built completely in Flash. Nike knows that their audience is technically proficient enough to have the latest browser or to update their plug-in if the latest version is not already installed. In contrast, L.L. Bean's website, gathering in a less cutting-edge technical audience, uses plug-ins only to enhance their content. There are no roadblocks to prevent her from having a satisfying, easy shopping experience—even if her system is missing some of the bells and whistles tech-raised twixters covet. Both of these companies knew who was going to be using their site (and why), long before they coded their first html tag.

3. Grow with Her

The days of a website simply being a collection of linked static pages that Baby Boomer women hop to and from, are gone. The Web now offers the potential for a customized, personalized, fluid relationship. It's a unique medium that has the ability to interact with your audience like no other.

YogaJournal.com, the most comprehensive yoga portal for everything from novices to yoga teachers, is an example of this, with over 450,000 visitors a month. Though the typical yoga practitioner is a 40-year-old female, yoga's popularity spans a wide range of ages and experience levels.[6] The site has established itself as a multi-experience destination by providing a deep Web experience that grows with the visitor over time. Considering that their users could be on any connection from dial-up to broadband, educational aspects of the site are offered in various formats, including streaming video, Flash, and static images—all with detailed descriptions. Without overwhelming, the site provides easy access to a wide audience by tailoring sections with content for beginners, experts, and teachers.

4. Send Your Message Home to Her—On Occasion

Permission e-mail can be a powerful tool—but only if it's used with care. Your e-mail should contain information she wants or needs. But be careful not to bombard her inbox. Don't send an e-mail every week with "ten new markdowns . . . buy one get one free," and other discounting programs. Using your e-mail marketing programs as a platform for liquidations is a sure way to erode her perception of your brand. Invasive frequency will eventually cause apathy with your communications, and she'll unsubscribe from your list. The biggest no-no: unsolicited e-mail.

5. Start a Buddy System

Fostering a sense of community is one important way to develop a website that connects with Baby Boomer women. And there is no better way to do this than to partner with someone who offers products or content that complements your brand and helps make it into a culture—a place for people to visit, share, learn, stay, and talk for a while.

Altrec.com is an example of a company that uses partnering as a way to build in value, of particular appeal to the Baby Boomer woman. This online retailer of outdoor gear not only offers all the accoutrements for almost any outdoor activity, but provides customer reviews and 360-degree video views with commentary on select products. They further enhance their brand's value by partnering with GreatOutdoors .com, which offers editorial content about outdoor adventuring. Altrec integrates relevant articles directly into the home pages for each unique activity.

In return, GreatOutdoors.com offers a gear search that loads product you've selected into an Altrec.com shopping cart. This enhanced experience transforms both of these Web presences from just separate sites to resources. Successful partnerships are more than simple reciprocal links. They impact your programming and user experience and need to be carefully planned in the beginning stages of development.

6. Establish and Maintain Trust

Make it easy for the Baby Boomer woman to find your privacy policy and security seals. Unlike most other segments of the population, she'll be looking! Too many companies hide privacy policies in obscure, hard-to-find areas of their websites, and yet privacy is a bigger concern for women than for men.

7. You Can Build It, But Will She Come?

Successful sites don't happen by chance. A compelling online experience geared toward women is developed with care and the understanding that she has to be considered from the very beginning of the website planning process. Remember, it's not just about getting her to visit you once. Rather, it's about making her want to build you into the fabric of her life.

Uni-Channel Marketing

Throughout this chapter, we've been navigating our way around the upside-down influencer hierarchy, where the consumer now calls the shots. The relational nature of the Internet is well-suited to this consumer-driven communications model. But as important as it is for the marketer to know how to use the Internet strategically with the Baby Boomer woman, the time has come to put this revolutionary communications channel into an even larger context.

For years, the big news among marketers has been perfecting integrated marketing communications programs utilizing multiple channels. Rather than thinking of the Web as an add-on, for example, companies instead began integrating their website presence into the overall marketing mix. Multichannel marketers learned that they could readily leverage a thirty-second radio or television advertisement into a ten-minute website visit. For the multitasking, multimedia Baby Boomer woman, who is watching television and reading the newspaper at the same time, who leaves at the commercial break to check her e-mails and answer the phone (or hang up on a telemarketer), it is a giant step forward to make your brand experience available to her via multiple channels.

Just as the field of marketing has advanced from single-channel thinking to multichannel strategies, the next step will be towards what we refer to as the "Uni-Channel Marketing Universe." Even as we are writing this chapter, information systems that are far more evolved than the World Wide Web are taking form in technology labs around the world.

Every aspect of communication in our lives—cell and landline phones, libraries and research, bill-paying, satellite TV, GPS navigations, entertainment, financial transactions, health monitoring, and shopping—are already bursting through the boundaries of multichannel layering to become one all-encompassing, 360-degree, 3-D channel.[7] It is no longer sufficient that multichannel marketing communications vehicles be simply "integrated" with one another. We're also talking about how and where goods are sold, who and how customer service is delivered, what her friends and strangers are saying about it, and even what are the unconscious influences that make her feel one way or another about any particular company or product. In other words, the consumer experience will be taken as a whole: the lines between product, distribution, and marketing will be erased.

Moving Across Channels

The demand upon the marketer is to view all consumer touchpoints, regardless of channel, as essentially the same communication. If you're not communicating core values and experiences uniformly through all your channels, she'll experience a disconnect.

Moreover, your brand must move with her from one channel experience to another seamlessly.

As an example, Progressive Auto Insurance raised the "uni-channel" bar when they figured out a way to move the consumer from television ad to their website for an online quote. Along the way, the Baby Boomer woman, who is more often than not making the purchasing decision concerning various kinds of insurances for herself and her family, has been empowered—at one touch of her pinky—to be seamlessly connected to a live, licensed expeditor. The company representative can pick up with her mid-transaction, should the consumer become confused, knowing exactly where she left off without skipping a beat.

Catalog and retail giant JC Penney is another company that understands the importance of uni-channel marketing. Enter your zip code on JCPenney.com and you can instantaneously browse through your local JC Penney store's sales flyer, download coupons, order a print catalog to be mailed to your home, or flip through one online. Items purchased through any channel can be returned or exchanged via any channel. In other words, the customer can return an item bought online to a JC Penney location.

No longer is the Baby Boomer woman penalized for stepping outside her comfort zone. This challenges the retailer, of course. But it's not the Baby Boomer woman's job to understand how the retailer's business works. Not only is it not a matter of understanding—she doesn't care. She wants what she wants, when she wants it, the way she wants it. At any touch-point of the brand, the consumer finds a consistent experience—and it's got to be the experience she is looking for.

Making Waves

As we have seen in this chapter, the Baby Boomer woman has already found her way to connecting to others—despite being ignored by the mainstream media. Her preferences (and gripes) sweep through her complex and extensive web of relationships like waves across the ocean. With the click of her mouse, she is once again leading a societal revolution, overturning the stereotypes of aging to reinvent the role of women 40+ in the consumer marketplace. This, then, is the new brandscape for marketers, and there's no turning back the clock. Wake up, and rethink the channels of communication that will help you connect with who really has control over the economic purse strings and you, too, can become a serious player in the world's largest and most lucrative consumer segment.

CHAPTER SEVEN

She's Waiting

The Marketer's Call to Action

Throughout the course of this book, we've been hearing directly from many experienced marketers, a number of whom are Boomers. Both in their formal essays, and in the conversations with us that preceded and followed, some common themes have surfaced.

In the foreword to this book, Paco Underhill set the tone by noting that the time is ripe for a book that takes marketing to this segment of the population seriously. The majority of our contributors join in his challenge to the marketing community "to wake up and rethink just who it is that has control over the economic purse strings." Of course, by now you know it's the Baby Boomer woman. But always keep in mind, as our experts repeatedly warn us, that in truth, there's no such thing as "The" Baby Boomer woman. Rather, Baby Boomer women are a complex and challenging cohort, spanning 18 years, a number of life stages and influences.

If this weren't challenging enough, a number of our contributors, from Thermador and Ford, to Appleseed's and Time Inc., have pointed out the importance of taking a deep dive into the very heart of her psyche, onto the largely unmapped territory of motivational marketing. The Imago Diagnostic ("ID") that we shared with you in Chapter Four guides marketers to identify a primary motivational archetype of their target consumer, capturing the richness, complexity, and depth of who she is. The three archetypes—Conventional, Transitional, and Aspirational Boomer woman—provide the context that will help get the tone just right with her, building relevant, strategic messages into the core of your communications.

The Facts Speak for Themselves

In industry after industry, the light is dawning that it is the woman of the Baby Boomer generation who is the chief purchasing officer not only for herself, but for her extended network of relationships. Moreover, this woman is defying the stereotype that by the time she reaches midlife and beyond, her brand preferences and purchasing behaviors are set in stone. This is a generation of women who have been bringing innovative thinking and problem-solving strategies to every stage of their lives. The challenges and opportunities at midlife and beyond are proving to be no exception to the rule.

On Redressing the Misconceptions

Dorothy Dowling,

Senior Vice President of Marketing

BEST WESTERN INTERNATIONAL

The hospitality industry is only just now recognizing the tremendous opportunity that the financial power, knowledge, and interest in travel among Baby Boomer women represents for us. Until recently, there's been the misconception that consumers' brand preferences are locked in by the time they reach 40. But research today shows that Boomers are more willing to brand-hop than younger consumers.

At the same time, it is important to keep in mind the tremendous diversity within this demographic. To put this in perspective, Boomer women range from their early 40s to early 60s. They could be single, married, or divorced. Some have children in diapers, while others are grandparents. Given this reality, the marketing industry has yet to fully capitalize on the female Boomer market opportunity.

The key is to define the subsegments and focus on reaching the individual with messages she wants to hear. At Best Western, we're marketing to lifecycle, rather than age, reaching them with relevant messages based on the information they've provided and their booking patterns. We're also identifying appropriate promotional partners, special amenities and vacation packages that will appeal to the individual. We're striving to do more direct marketing to Boomer women in this way.

I want to see marketers give Boomer women products and offers that reflect and enable them to express who they really are. This includes acknowledging what is life stage-appropriate while conveying a youthful sensibility. It means creating products with the right mix of image, performance, relevance and simplicity that accommodate and respond to the many demands on her time.

Dorothy Dowling brings with her more than twenty years of experience within the hospitality and travel industries. At Best Western, Dowling directs the execution and delivery of all brand marketing strategies, including frequency, consumer, and field marketing programs, advertising/creative services, public relations, and e-commerce initiatives. Previously,

Dowling was vice president of operations, Parks & Resorts, for ARAMARK. Dowling serves on the North American and international boards of Hospitality Sales & Marketing Association International (HSMAI) and on the North American board for the Travel Industry Association of America (TIA). Dowling has received the American Hotel Foundation Award for Best Practices in Guest Loyalty Programs.

Early Adopters

Marketers who have been early adopters of initiatives directed to the Baby Boomer woman have discovered that if they have a product or service that will help her solve a problem, they've got a potential winner on their hands. At the same time, most agree that while she is eager to be acknowledged by companies and in the media, she is no pushover. As a decision maker, she tends to be more demanding than her male counterpart, paying exceptional attention to value, details, as well as quality of service relationships. To the marketers who worry that in appealing to her they may lose their male consumer, the message that has come through loud and clear is this: Satisfy her needs, and more often then not you will exceed the expectations of the other demographics as well, increasing your share of segments across the board.

Focusing on marketing to Baby Boomer women, instead of the historically sought-after demographic of choice, 18- to 34-year olds, is no less than a marketplace revolution, turning the consumer desirability formula upside down. This reframing of the coveted demographic is synergistically connected to the inverted hierarchy of communication channels developing in the twenty-first century. In the new consumer brandscape, it is no longer traditional media or top-down authorities carrying the weight. In fact, her skepticism of the advertising and marketing industry on the whole is at an all-time high as marketers continue to miss the mark with middle-aged women.

In the new upside-down influencer hierarchy, it is the Baby Boomer woman herself who is calling the shots in terms of what information she is seeking and whom she will allow into her life. The realm of public relations, in cultivating word-of-mouth, editorial, event, and educational opportunities, is increasingly becoming more effective in cutting through the hype and getting your brand in front of Boomer women.

The New Marketing Universe

Welcome to the emerging uni-channel marketing universe, where customers no longer perceive their experience with brands as channel specific, but as one-continuous touch-point experience. In this universe, if you are not integrating and translating your core brand messages consistently, regardless of channel, you'll lose the Baby Boomer woman. She has no tolerance for lack of attention to detail or inconsistency of communication. To her, that's a recipe for a bad relationship. Admittedly, this uni-channel model is new territory for marketers, and our contributors have been candid about both sharing the experience of their successes—and guiding others on how to avoid the pitfalls.

Recall Fran Philip, chief merchandising officer of L.L. Bean, who warns us to resist the urge to "just shrink it and pink it." Marketers who hope to cut corners with the Baby Boomer woman by taking a product designed for men, cutting it down in size, and putting frills on it, won't cut it with this discerning consumer if the product doesn't meet her needs. You've got to listen to her, making sure the products and services you deliver provide a real solution for her.

Design a product that offers her exactly what she needs, and you can still fall flat with her, if, for example, the booklet that accompanies it offers instructions in type too small for her bifocaled eyes to read. Kathy Moyer Dragon, the founder of the Dragon's Path and ActiveWomen.com, reminds us that when a travel brochure arrives in the mail, the Boomer woman also notices how the envelope was addressed and whether it was handwritten or mass mailed. "When they call or e-mail the company, they care how the phone was answered (hopefully directly by a real person). They want to talk to someone who listens to them and asks question, calms their fears, encourages them, speaks informatively."

Inspiring us all are the happy surprises of expectations not only met, but exceeded. Rose Rodd, director of marketing for Palm, Inc., shared the keys to success that unlocked the Baby Boomer woman consumer for the Palm Zire. "We learned that the heaviest users of the Zire handheld were somewhat older than we expected, at 35 to 55 years of age. At the core of this demographic were the women of the Baby Boomer generation." One of the keys to Palm's success: the decision to sell the "real world benefits" of the Zire organizer, not sell the technology. "That made all the difference for women who understood what the improvement the Zire would be over sticky yellow note-laden Filofaxes."

More magazine, targeting women 40 to 60 years old, has more than tripled their circulation since the turn of the century. What they've discovered as the secret of reaching their demographic: "When we put attractive, successful women on our covers who look like they are between their late 40s and mid 50s, we sell lots more copies than when we go for the '40, could pass for 32' look. . . . Our readers want to be able to see what these faces really look like. And they see something they like: a knowing quality, a sense of confidence. It's reassurance that the coming decades are an open door, not a barrier," say Editor-in-Chief Peggy Northrop and Publisher Brenda Saget Darling.

And who would have thought that Baby Boomer women would

prove to be an important market for motor scooters? "People may be surprised to hear that Boomers represent 40 percent of the Vespa market, with women representing a large share of this segment," says Federico Musi, vice president of marketing for Vespa, North America. Why? "She sees a Vespa as a reward for all that she's accomplished. After years of delayed gratification, parenting, working hard, taking care of others, she's ready to explore new dimensions of life. Now she's on a quest, fulfilling lifelong desires such as traveling, writing, and spirituality. She is, in fact, expressing her full power."

Beyond the strategies, insights, and successes of our contributors, however, another theme emerged from our conversations: the almost missionary zeal with which many approach the subject of understanding and reaching Boomer women. One of the questions we asked our contributors to address was this: "What personal requests/hopes/advice do you have concerning how you would like to see this group addressed? What kind of positive impact could this have on you, the business community, the world?" The cumulative response was remarkably unified and powerful, constituting no less than a call to action, which we heartily join and support. This call is directed to five audiences.

Call to Action: *Marketing Directors*

The first call to action is to marketing directors of companies and organizations. Marketers have historically looked to the younger crowd for inspiration and indicators of hot future trends. But now take into account the fact that the average American woman is living about thirty years longer than she did 100 years ago. If the brands and services aimed at this consumer continue to rely on the stereotypical notions of older as an un-cool, has-been demographic, they'll perish.

As Christopher Bradley of Cuddledown, who has served as president of the New England Mail Order Association, points out, these stereotypes are particularly resistant in organizations led by younger marketers who are emotionally attracted to targeting members of their own or younger generations.

On Getting Past Emotional Bias

Christopher W. Bradley,
President and Chief Executive Officer

CUDDLEDOWN INC.

The track record of American marketing's effort to capture the attention of Baby Boomer women has been mixed. The massive buying power and purchasing control represented by Baby Boomer women dominates our economy, yet many marketers, distracted by the glamour of younger generations, package their message in such a way as to make it hard for Baby Boomers to relate. Even though Baby Boomer women control the purse strings, advertisements featuring 40+ models (Christie Brinkley, Andie MacDowell, Susan Sarandon, Julianne Moore, Jamie Lee Curtis) are the exception rather than the rule.

Many direct marketing companies are staffed by people under the age of 40 whose creative styles seem more inspired by MTV than NBC. These marketers are often not members of the target market, so the connection is harder to make. The result is that many companies ignore the buying power of the Baby Boomer woman, and instead go after a younger demographic that they find more attractive. I would argue that this is an emotional decision, and it shortchanges both the marketer and the market.

Christopher W. Bradley formed an investor group to acquire the Portland, Maine-based Cuddledown Inc. in 1988. He transformed the company into a premier national catalog retailer of luxury bedding, sleep apparel, and home furnishings. Prior to Cuddledown, Bradley worked in New York City for Shearson Lehman Brothers and Chase Manhattan Bank. He holds a bachelor's degree from Colby College and an MBA from the University of Utah.

Beyond the Maverick

We challenge brand stewards of all ages to explore the dynamic, trend-setting potential of the Baby Boomer woman powerhouse. Once the marketer understands the importance of marketing to this demographic, the next challenge is to resist the urge of thinking of her as a niche. For most consumer industries, she is, in truth, the very heart and soul of the marketplace.

On Moving Beyond the Holy Grail

Ira Mayer,

President and Publisher, Marketing to Women

EPM COMMUNICATIONS

Baby Boomers don't like to feel neglected. As Lisa Finn wrote in our monthly newsletter, *Marketing to Women*, "Baby

Boomers have been the center of attention for a long time. . . . As they pass out of the coveted 18 to 49 demographic, many are feeling left out, and frustrated that marketers and entertainment companies are no longer clamoring for their attention."

When I speak to groups, I like to point out that under-30s say 67 is "old." Those over 60 say 76.5 is "old." And the average life expectancy is 76. So most people will be dead for six months before they get old! Truth is, women are working longer often out of necessity, but also because it feeds their vitality and self-image in very positive ways. And their multitasking, networking, and other skills and experience are highly valued, as well they should be.

The opportunity is enormous for entertainment, packaged goods, and services, among others. This is a group that is accustomed to paying for convenience, if marketers let go of 18 to 49 as the Holy Grail. (Of course, most marketers are too young to care, which has long been an issue.)

Show Boomer women as they are, in all their diversity. Don't talk to them or treat them as though they're has-beens. And most of all, listen. They'll tell you everything you need to know about developing products and services, advertising, and marketing to them. They'll appreciate the opportunity, and if you get it right, they'll be loyal. For a long time!

Ira Mayer is publisher of EPM Communications' monthly newsletter, *Marketing to Women*, and speaks frequently on consumer trends. To download a sample issue of the newsletter, please visit www.epmcom.com/mtw.

Call to Action: *Corporations*

The second call to action we issue is to the corporations themselves, to stop looking at the forward-thinking marketer in their midst—the one who recognizes the importance of Baby Boomer women—as a maverick. Rather, we call on the highest levels of corporate and organizational life to recognize him or her as a thought-leader who is working smart, ensuring that the brand will remain competitive. Marketing to Baby Boomer women should no longer have to be the realm of the lone demographic champion, upsetting the status quo at his or her peril. The commitment from corporate must be strong, flowing through to the very core of the organization, reinforcing the revolutionary notion that marketing to the Baby Boomer woman is not simply an initiative, but rather an intrinsic part of the company's means of doing business.

Call to Action: *Boomer Women Executives*

The third call to action is specifically directed to Baby Boomer women who are in positions of power in marketing agencies and corporations, as well as in the media. We know, better than anybody, our ability to make things happen for ourselves. Many of us are recognizing the beginning of a grassroots movement within these circles of power, with women of this generation refusing to be marginalized and to play to the stereotypes of what it means to be a female over 40 years old in the workplace. This includes taking a stand for ourselves professionally, as well as finding the opportunities to speak the truth concerning the potential of the women of the Baby Boomer generation as productive consumers. It takes courage to demand products and services, as well as the images and messaging that buck what Ira Mayer calls "The Holy Grail." Do so, and you will emerge with a previously untapped source of revenue under your belt. At the same time, you will be helping to create the infrastructure for a society that is appropriately respectful of who women are as we age, providing us with the products and services we need, as well as supporting the media and other means of communication that connect us to one another.

On the Evolution of Marketing to the Baby Boomer Woman

Lori Bitter,

Partner and Business Development Director

J. WALTER THOMPSON, MATURE MARKET GROUP

Twenty years ago, Boomer futurist Ken Dychtwald began sharing this metaphor with his audiences (and I paraphrase): "Picture the Baby Boomer generation as an elephant stampeding through the jungle: Will you get out in front of it and dig a big trench . . . or will you run behind it shooting arrows at its butt?"

I would assert that as marketers we didn't dig a trench; we have not even run behind the Boomer female. We were trampled and did not even know what hit us! What is fascinating is that the failure to advance the notion of "women as the primary purchasers of damn near everything" has occurred in tandem with the ranks of the advertising/marketing professions swelling with Boomer women. Have we somehow betrayed ourselves? How is it that in the last several years, we have finally grabbed the bow and quiver and begun shooting like crazy as the earth rumbles under her stampeding feet?

Simplistically, I believe that a couple of things happened to us in the workplace that kept us from trusting our insights into ourselves as the power consumers we are. As women, we "know" things *intuitively*; things that men will demand research to validate. The very notion of intuition has been so ridiculed in the media that women shy away from even acknowledging its presence and importance in our daily lives.

That said, you don't build a profit plan on "gut." You do build it on numbers. The basic census data to validate the size and arrival of the Boomer consumer, and consequently the female Boomer consumer, has been available for years.

When I talk to women about how we got here, I get amazing perspective. There is a segment of women at the top of the advertising/marketing field that I call "early achievers." They are the Boomer women who scraped their way to the top, clutching *Ms.* magazine, and kicking through the barriers for us middle Boomers. Overwhelmingly their supervisors were men whose best interests were not served by creating sweeping change in marketing perspective. In the midst of this cultural gender evolution (and chaos) in marketing organizations, the image of the Boomer female consumer did not evolve. She remained shaped as the aging mother of guys at the head of marketing, regardless of the women in the meetings.

Then a second wave of women in marketing emerged. These middle Boomer women hired and managed younger women and their peers. Instead of using our native gifts and creating intuitive, collaborative environments where the woman consumer would naturally emerge from their collective energy, these women became the working woman's worst enemy. In their struggle to stay on top and in their power roles, these women killed their potential to enlighten and lead their organizations and shape the future of many great brands.

These environments made lasting impressions on many of us. We either found our voice or left the field. We figured out that emulating men in the workplace robs us of the value we bring to the table—intuition and insight. And our ideas have emerged in full voice with the numbers to support them.

Our personal frustration and problem-solver personalities have emboldened us. Some of us have left the marketing/advertising field and created businesses to serve our peers. Others of us went to the client side of the business to try to solve the problem from within. A few brave cohorts launched out on their own to create agencies and consultancies to put the female consumer out front and top of mind for brands worldwide.

Next, two women: Martha and Oprah. Seriously. These Boomer icons showed us how to value and express our authentic selves, and the power of aspiration. In some way, they give us permission to validate our intuition. Not to be goofy, but we have learned the awesomeness of being women. This theme of connection can be translated into a powerful marketing tool that extends perfectly to the Internet for savvy marketers.

Finally, demographics don't lie. Marketers of nearly every product category are waking up (too late for many) to the sheer number of Boomer women in the marketplace, and they are realizing that they have ignored us at their peril. The financial power of this "segment" is now clearly understood and undeniable. Brand leaders are emerging and will profit from our attraction and loyalty.

The real frontier is the serum on the arrowhead: relevant, compelling, and entertaining messaging for smart women, and by extension, discovering the touch points for our products and the resulting media opportunities that compel Boomer women to spend time with our brands. Most companies did not dig the trench that Dychtwald prescribed years ago. Consequently we are destined to slinging arrows at the elephant's butt. Thank God the target is huge.

Lori Bitter is responsible for the strategic development and execution of consumer-focused marketing plans to J. Walter Thompson's Mature Market Group team. Formerly senior vice president/director of client services for Age Wave Impact, Lori has more than twenty years of advertising, public relations, and strategic planning experience, working for clients such as AOL, Listerine, and IBM. In her role at Mature Market Group, Lori manages the production of "Beyond the Numbers—The Mature Market Summit," now in its fifth year. She is editor of *LiveWire*, the quarterly publication of the Mature Market Group, and author of numerous white papers on topics relevant to the senior and Boomer population.

Call to Action: *Women Baby Boomers, Themselves*

Our fourth call to action is to the women of the Baby Boomer generation, marketers or not, who must prepare to rise to this next occasion life is bringing our way. Part of this involves refusing to settle for any less than the attention and respect we deserve from corporate America. Caleb Mason of DeLorme reminds us of our history and impact. "Hers was the first generation of women to enter the workforce in large numbers. This new economic freedom allowed women to define the rules of trade in ways that would have been unthinkable back in the 1950s. This was a generation of women who were on a mission: the busy female worker who was doing her best to balance career with motherhood. Helping her rise to the time-related challenges of "having it all" led to all sorts of marketing creativity. From the express checkout line at supermarkets and drive-through prescriptions and banking, to store-within-a-store mall concepts that brought different goods under one roof. All of these were driven by the female Baby Boomer's need and ability to pay for convenience."

As Caleb Mason looks toward the future, he sees the potential for this generation of women to bring innovation once again, not only to the marketplace, but to society as a whole. Baby Boomer women would not be where they are today without their efforts to break down old social, economic, and political barriers.

"It annoys me when their history is portrayed by younger generations as having been a time of irresponsible hedonism," Mason states. "Showing advertising that captures the courage of those who fought for social change will help sell products. Moreover, by appealing to the nostalgia value for the generation's legacy, it will inspire them to revisit their history of social activism. I believe that the Boomers, as they age and mellow, will get back to concerns of conservation and responsible environmentalism. They will create a demand for products that will enable our dependence on existing fuel sources to diminish. This is the true definition of being empowered."

Caleb Mason's message regarding this generation's legacy was echoed by a number of our contributors. Bill Novelli, CEO of AARP, sees in Baby Boomer women the potential for a new generation of activists, ready to potently address the challenges of a society that is growing older. Will Baby Boomer women, with their better education and heightened motivation, pool their resources and get involved politically, economically, and socially? "The message has got to be communicated that by working together to fulfill the promise that longevity offers, the larger society will benefit as well," Novelli concludes.

The Final Call: *Market Researchers*

Our fifth and final call is to researchers in the social sciences, including the fields of marketing and communications, who need to continue to study the largely unmapped territory of adult development. The psychosocial model we shared in Chapter Four fills in some of the gaps of traditional adult development theory. This research is just a beginning, however, highlighting the need to expand existing models of adult development and their applicability to marketers hoping to understand the potentialities of the unprecedented life spans, complex motivations, and heightened aspirations of this generation of women, as well as generations to come. Regardless of at what life stage or psychosocial stage the Baby Boomer woman may be in her dynamic transit through the years pre- and post-menopause, her journey through midlife and beyond is turning out to be a far cry from the developmental wasteland both scholars and marketers once thought this period of a woman's life represented. Rather, our research points the way to an experience-rich opportunity for marketers to tap into the unprecedented wealth of this surprisingly dynamic generation throughout the course of their adult lives.

Women over 40 were once virtually invisible to marketers, believed to be entrenched in habitual, staid shopping patterns, and enmeshed with their favorite brands. Nothing could be further from the truth. In these super-charged times, where we experience a technology or communication revolution daily, all the traditional marketing adages are being called on the carpet. As Paco Underhill suggests, in this climate of challenge and change, follow the money toward the resilient consumer, motivated and able to navigate her way through unmapped territory to get what she wants. More often than not, this wise and determined consumer will be a woman of the Baby Boomer generation.

These are exciting times to be a woman 40+. She has never been more powerful, more creative, and more demanding. Get in sync with her, and these can be equally exciting times to be a marketer as well.

Our final words of advice to you: Wake up, and rethink this demographic, and you, too, will be in the position to grow your market share of today's most powerful consumer. It's time to get started. After all, she's waiting!

NOTES

Introduction

1. Russell, Cheryl. *The Baby Boom: Americans Born 1946–1964.* New York: New Strategist, 4th Edition—The American Generations Series, p. 218, 2004.

Chapter One

1. "Demographic Profile of American Baby Boomers." MetLife Mature Market Institute, 2005.

2. U.S. Census Bureau, 2000.

3. Japanese Baby Boomer information gathered from a February 15, 2006 e-mail exchange with I. Fujita International, Inc. Generally speaking, the Baby Boomer population in Japan falls into the age

category of 40s to 50s. The major issue in Japan is that this aging population will be creating a major senior market in years to come. Consumer-related businesses can no longer afford to ignore this demographic. Baby Boomers in Japan have solid financial assets and have high purchasing power. Some of the trends found in Japanese Baby Boomers are:

- Taking tours customized for their own generation
- Buying outdoor goods
- Embracing consumer electronics
- Going to aesthetic salons
- Ordering home delivery meals from luxury hotel restaurants
- Hiring service companies to do their house cleaning
- Going to movies, concerts and presentations
- Buying fashionable outer and undergarments
- Purchasing sporty small engine displacement automobiles
- Going to the gym
- Hiring contractors to refurbish their homes and buying high-end home theaters

There are many companies in Japan that have started focusing on the female Baby Boomer market. For example, the apparel company called Kanebo and Onward Kashiyama are now designing "young-oriented" clothing for mid-age and older Japanese women. Onward Kashiyama has developed a brand called "Jane Moore" specifically for women in their mid- to late-50s.

4. David K. Foot, *Boom Bust and Echo 2000: Profiting from the New Millennium.* Don Mills, Ontario: Stoddart Publishing, 2001.

5. U.S. Census Bureau, 2000.

6. Russell, Cheryl. *The Baby Boom: Americans Born 1946–1964,* 4th Edition. New York: New Strategist, 2004, p. 218.

7. Bureau of Labor Statistics, *Consumer Expenditure Survey*, 2003.

8. Ken Dychtwald. *Age Power.* New York: Penguin Putnam, 2000.

9. Reported in *Fast Company Magazine*, March 2004, by David Wolfe, author of *Ageless Marketing.*

10. "Women and Finance Project." Simmons Market Research and marketresearch.com, January 3, 2002.

11. Marilyn Edelson, *Gender-Specific Relationship-Building Grows Power, Market Share.* Posted on BostonHerald.com. Sourced by U.S. Census Bureau.

12. "Demographic Profile of American Baby Boomers," MetLife Mature Market Institute, 2005.

13. AARP, 2005.

14. Bureau of Labor Statistics, *American Demographics*, March 2003.

15. U.S. Census Bureau, 2000.

16. Lowe's *Survey*, 2003.

17. Business Women's Network. *WOW! Facts 2004*: *U.S. Multicultural and Global Markets.* Washington, D.C: Diversity Best Practices, 2004.

18. *American Women. Who They Are and How They Live*, 2nd edition. Ithaca, N.Y.: New Strategist Publications, 2002.

19. Nielsen/Net Ratings, 2004.

20. Ken Burke. *Media Live*, 2004.

21. Center for Women's Business Research, 2004.

22. Ibid.

23. National Association of Women Business Owners, 2006.

24. Coming of Age, Inc. www.comingofage.com.

25. Based on research paper by Drs. Carol Orsborn and Jimmy

Laura Smull, presented at fall Colloquium for UCLA's Center for the Study of Religion, October 5, 2005, Los Angeles California. Dr. Myrna Hant, respondant.

26. National Center for Health Statistics. *Vital Statistics of the United States*, Volume II, 2002.

Chapter Two

1. Figure 2-1 builds on a conceptual framework provided by the Mature Market Group, a division of J. Walter Thompson Worldwide, New York, 2004.

2. U.S. Census Bureau, 2000.

3. *Os-Cal Wellness Matters: A Magazine for Healthy Living*, 2005.

Chapter Three

1. Imago Creative commissioned the application of the Orsborn/Smull Study for marketing purposes and co-sponsored the day with the authors.

2. Imago Creative, *Empty Nest Survey*, consisting of a survey of 230 pre- and current-empty nester women. Survey conducted online with BoomerWomenSpeak.com, and supported by the Orsborn/Smull qualitative study as well as other sources, 2005.

3. Imago Creative, *Empty Nest Survey*, 2005.

4. General Mills Press Release: "Pillsbury® Takes Baby Boomers from Full House to Empty Nest. Trusted brand launches wide-ranging 'Cooking for Two' campaign, beginning with AARP National Event, aimed at helping empty nesters." October 12, 2004.

5. Imago Creative, *Empty Nest Survey*, 2005.

6. "The Evolving Summer Marketplace." *Leisure Trak* Report, 2004.

7. *Yoga Journal Survey,* 2005.

8. "Fastest Growing Franchise." *Entrepreneur* magazine, 2005. Posted on money.cnn.com.

9. Mattingly, Marybeth and Liana Sayer. As sourced in Suzanne Bianchi and Sara Raley, "Changing Work and Family Demographics, 2003.

10. "Baby Boomer Women: Reshaping Themselves and Their Future." W2W, a division of Campbell-Ewald, 2005.

11. Avon's *Global Women's Survey*, 2003.

12. American Society of Plastic Surgeons, 2002.

13. Harris Interactive Study, 2000.

14. U.S. Census Bureau, 2002.

15. Ibid, 2000.

16. Women's Financial Network at Siebert, 2005.

17. Ibid, 2002.

18. Center for Women's Business Research, 2004.

19. Ibid.

20. U.S. Department of Labor. Women's Bureau, 2004. www.dol.gov/wb.

21. AARP, 2002.

22. Ibid.

23. National Center on Women and Aging, 2002.

24. Pew Internet and American Life Project, June 2004.

25. Ibid, 2005.

26. Published in *WOW! U.S. Women's Market.* Sourced by Reimagine, Tom Peters, 2003.

27. Travel Industry Association of America (TIA). *Domestic Travel Market Report*, 2002.

28. Ibid, 2003 Edition. www.tia.org.

29. Marybeth Bond of *CA Tourism Insight* magazine, 2006. Womentraveltips.com.

30. ActiveWomen.com. Kathy Moyer Dragon, president.

31. International Spa Association, 2002-2003.

32. Travel Industry Association of America (TIA). *Domestic Travel Market Report*, 2003 Edition. www.tia.org.

33. Home Improvement Research Industry, 2005.

34. National Women's Health Resource Center. "Women Talk." *Marketing to Women* Newsletter, Volume 18, July 2005.

35. Harris Interactive for Susan Komen Foundation. www.komen.org.

36. Millaward Brown Intelliquest, April 16, 2001.

37. eMarketer. "Women Online in the US," April 7, 2005.

38. Nielsen/Net Ratings, 2004.

39. Pew Internet and American Life Project, December 28, 2005.

40. comScore Media Metrix. *The Score*, February 6, 2003.

41. Pew Internet and American Life Project, December 28, 2005.

42. People Support. www.peoplesupport.com.

43. Frank About Women, February 4, 2004. www.frankaboutwomen.com.

Chapter Four

1. Frank About Women. www.frankaboutwomen.com.
2. AARP. *The Magazine*, July/August 2004.
3. *New York Times Book Review*, February 5, 2006.

Chapter Five

1. The five phases are based on the standard five-stage model of the consumer buying process, as outlined by Professor Philip Kotler in his best-selling marketing textbook, *Principles of Marketing,* 11th edition. Upper Saddle River, N.J.: Prentice Hall, 2005.

2. Frank About Women. "Elevated Expectations: The New Female Value Equation," 2004. www.frankaboutwomen.com.

Chapter Six

1. Direct Selling Association Industry Statistics, 2004.
2. *Inc.* magazine, 2004. www.tastefullysimple.com.
3. Pew Internet. "How Women and Men Use the Internet," 2005. www.pewinternet.org.
4. EPM Communications. *Marketing to Women* Newsletter, Volume 16 (July 2003), p. 6.
5. Johnson, Lisa and Andrea Learned. *Don't Think Pink*. New York: AMACOM, 2004. Chapter 9, "The Internet-Savvy Woman."
6. YogaJournal.com.
7. From a presentation by Donald Libey, a leading direct marketing and catalog industry futurist.

RESOURCES

Recommended Reading

A brief compendium of resources and information that we have found invaluable in understanding and studying the topic of marketing to women of the Baby Boomer generation.

Marketing to Women

Books

Barletta, Martha. *Marketing to Women: How to Understand, Reach, and Increase your Share of the World's Largest Market Segment,* 2nd Edition. Chicago: Kaplan Education, 2006.

Johnson, Lisa and Andrea Learned. *Don't Think Pink: What Really Makes Women Buy—and How to Increase Your Share of This Crucial Market.* New York: AMACOM, 2004.

Lake, Celinda and Kellyanne Conway, Catherine Whitney. *What Women Really Want: How American Women Are Quietly Erasing Political, Racial, Class, and Religious Lines to Change the Way We Live.* New York: Free Press, 2005.

Popcorn, Faith, and Lys Marigold. *EVEolution.* New York: Hyperion, 2000.

Quinlan, Mary Lou. *Just Ask a Woman: Cracking the Code of What Women Want and How They Buy.* New York: John Wiley & Sons, 2003.

Underhill, Paco. *Why We Buy: The Science of Shopping.* New York: Simon & Schuster, 2000.

———. *Call of the Mall: The Geography of Shopping.* New York: Simon & Schuster, 2004.

Yaccato, Joanne Thomas. *The 80% Minority: Reaching the Real World of Women Consumers.* Canada: Viking, 2003.

Newsletters/Blogs

Marketing to Women, monthly newsletter published by EMP Communications, New York. Covers news, trends, and research on marketing to women.

LearnedonWomen.com/blog.asp, weblog by Andrea Learned. Research and analysis of women's market efforts.

Michelemiller.blogs.com, weblog by Michelle Miller. Concepts, principles, and news on marketing to women.

Marketing to Baby Boomers

Books

Gillon, Steve. *Boomer Nation: The Largest and Richest Generation Ever, and How It Changed America.* New York: Free Press, 2004

Dychtwald, Ken and Joe Flower. *The Age Wave: How the Most Important Trend of Our Time Can Change Your Future.* New York: Bantam, 1990.

Wolfe, David B. and Robert Snyder. *Ageless Marketing: Strategies for Reaching the Hearts and Minds of the New Customer Majority*. Chicago: Kaplan Education, 2003.

Newsletters/Blogs

BoomerProject.com/current.html, monthly e-newsletter published by Matt Thornhill, Washington, D.C. Covers news and research on Boomers over 50.

LiveWire, The Newsletter: Resources for Reaching Mature Consumers, quarterly newsletter published by the Mature Market Group, a division of J. Walter Thompson Worldwide, New York.

Mature Marketing, monthly newsletter published by Buchan Publishing, Ltd., England. Covers trends, research, and intelligence on the "over-50" market.

Marketing to Baby Boomer Women

Newsletters

Femail Focus, monthly e-newsletter published by Imago Creative, Portland, Maine. Covers news, trends, research, and intelligence on marketing to Baby Boomer women.

Adult Development

Books

Bridges, William. *Transitions: Making Sense of Life's Changes.* New York: Perseus Book Publishing, 1980.

Erikson, Erik. *Identity: Youth and Crisis.* New York: W. W. Norton, 1968.

Erikson, Joan. *Wisdom and the Senses.* New York: W. W. Norton, 1988.

Feinstein, D. and S. Krippner. *Personal Mythology: The Psychology of Your Evolving Self.* Los Angeles: Jeremy P. Tarcher, 1988.

Fowler, J.W. *Stages of Faith: The Psychology of Human Development and the Quest for Meaning.* New York: Harper & Row, 1981.

Levinson, Daniel. *Seasons of a Man's Life* (edited by Charlotte N. Dorrow, Edward B. Klein, Maria H. Levinson, and Braxton McKee). New York: Alfred A. Knopf, 1978.

Orsborn, Carol and Jimmy Laura Smull. *The Silver Pearl: Our Generation's Journey to Wisdom.* Chicago: Ampersand Publishing, 2005.

Piaget, Jean. *The Construction of Reality in the Child* (M. Cook, trans.). New York: Basic Books, 1954.

Sheehy, Gail. *New Passages: Mapping Your Life Across Time.* New York: Random House, 1995.

Smull, Jimmy Laura. *Healing Eve: The Woman's Journey from Religious Fundamentalism to Religious Freedom.* Chicago: Ampersand Publishing, 2005.

INDEX

ABOUT THE AUTHORS

Mary Brown
President, Imago Creative, and Director, Boomer Women Marketing Group

As president of Imago Creative, Mary has distinguished herself as a leading voice on women as consumers. Imago Creative, the company she founded over a decade ago, has evolved into the only marketing firm in the United States to specialize in helping companies build brand relationships with women of the Baby Boomer generation. Mary is frequently sought as an industry expert, interviewed by the trade media and on National Public Radio (NPR), and hosting panels at industry conferences, such as the Boomer Marketing Summit. She is also a regular contributor to MarketingProfs.com. Mary studied humanities at Reed College in Portland, Oregon, followed by a BFA in photography from the San Francisco Art Institute.

Carol Orsborn, Ph.D.
Co-chair of FH Boom, and Senior Vice President, Fleishman-Hillard International Communications

A strategic communications veteran, Carol is the recipient of the Silver Anvil, the public relations industry's highest award. Carol has written fifteen books for and about women of the Baby Boom generation, leading to appearances on *The Today Show* and on *Oprah*. Her publications include *The Art of Resilience* (Three Rivers Press, a division of Random House); *Trust Inc.: A Practical Guide to the Alignment of Values, Organizational Goals and Results,* with coauthor Judith Rogala (www.TrustIncTheBook.Com); and *The Silver Pearl: Our Generation's Journey to Wisdom,* with coauthor Dr. Jimmy Laura Smull (www.TheSilverPearl.com). Carol is a research associate with UCLA. Her doctorate, in history and critical theory of religion, with specialization in the fields of ritual studies and adult development, is from Vanderbilt University.

* * *

To be part of the ongoing dialogue about marketing to women of the Baby Boomer generation, you are invited to subscribe to "Femail Focus," Imago Creative's e-newsletter, www.ImagoCreative.com, and to visit the FH Boom blog at www.TheBoomerBlog.com.